Sunlight through the Shadows

RITA TROTMAN

www.rollingdiceink.co.uk

First published in Great Britain by Rolling Dice Ink, 2013

This edition published by Rolling Dice Ink, 2013

Kindle Edition 2013

ISBN 978-0-9926347-0-4

All facts in this book are from diaries and the author's memory. Any inaccuracies are due entirely to the onset of old age.

www.rollingdiceink.co.uk

Acknowledgements

My husband Eric for love and support and for believing we could do it.

Neil and Rose Didlick, Betty Bailey, Tony and Deanne Dingley, Mo and Lee Springall for regular contributions.

Theo and Cath Armstrong for fundraising and friendship.

Angela Cowles for sharing the early years.

Isles of Scilly Rotary Club for generosity and support.

Isles of Scilly Methodist Church and the Isles of Scilly Parish Church for faith, fundraising and friendship.

Isles of Scilly Residents for rallying when the need was greatest.

Pam and Nick Kelson, Beryl and John Read, Terry and Jane Ward, William and Trish Thomas, Michelle and Steve Mapplethorpe and Steve Griffin for helping when it mattered most. Rob Courtice for IT support.

Eton College and the 'Pineapple Dames' for friendship and fundraising and the boys of Walpole House 1991-95.

Isles of Scilly Quilters for dedication and talent.

All unnamed supporters. You know who you are.

For Eric

and in loving memory of Aunt Pat

Chapter 1

I've been dozing fitfully, trying to sleep in foreign surroundings, immersed in unfamiliar heat. I'm tossing and turning, seeking non-existent coolness when a hideous scream shreds the night air. My heartbeat quickens; beads of sweat slick my skin and my mouth dries like a prune. There's no electricity, no necklace of sulphurous streetlights to illuminate the moment and no comforting hum of traffic. A short-lived silence momentarily calms the nerves, allows the pulse to settle. And then another harrowing scream. This one is shorter and muffled but nonetheless terrifying. I wish I wasn't in this place.

My room is dark as only rural habitation can be. The screech assaults my ears again and again. High pitched and regular, it's become rhythmic and now accompanied by deep, guttural breathing. The sickening cries fill a dark space close by. Worryingly, there is only the insignificant, shadowy thinness of a wall between us.

It's human anguish, of that I'm sure. No fox on heat ever attained such decibels. My senses define it, not from previous experience, but some primeval essence has welled up and names it for me. It's true fear. Not the horror movie kind, not the being chased by baddies type. This brand of fear creates a curdling of acid rather too low down for comfort. I breathe deeply, seeking oxygen. The frugal air gives up nothing but a stench of human despair. I'm thinking I haven't signed up for this.

'This' is the 'Let's have a month or two helping Romanian orphans,' impulse. A sentiment shared by thousands of people in the early nineties. And for many hundreds of us, from all over Europe, it became a reality. We'd seen the grotesque TV coverage of the orphanages; we'd learned of the tyrant Ceausescu and we flocked to help the underprivileged. All with a desire to help and our own particular path to tread. But my path, so far, was littered with piles of shit on stone floors and reams of Romanian red tape at every turn. And now, loud, inhuman screams in the night. Nothing in my past life had prepared me for this.

Earlier in the evening I'd crept outside the camine (orphanage) to wash. I'd closed the door to my room, wishing it had a lock, and made my way along the dark corridors. Thank heavens for my trusty torch. The night air was fresh with a fragrance of grass and musk from the horse tethered nearby. I recognised the gentle chomping of the camine's cow as she shuffled from one meagre, weedy tuft to the next, somewhere beyond the chain-link fencing. A screech owl rent the warm, night air - an oddly comforting sound of home.

Unfortunately, there'd been a heavy shower some time earlier and I found myself sliding in a top-coat of mud. Greasy and black, it squelched between toes and caked my sandals. There was a definite, unfamiliar odour to it.

A bucket of water hung from a large nail in the whitewashed wall and the content was my makeshift bathroom. The water was dingy brown and even by torchlight I could make out a layer of scum lurking on the surface. I couldn't raise a lather from my scented soap and as I held the fragrant tablet to my nose, thoughts of home nudged at me, seeking out a soft spot to torment. I fought the emotion, almost too much to bear at that moment. Bathrooms, flushing loos and running water; my much-loved sons ensconced in their warm beds; never would I take any of it for granted again.

I wasted no time. It was possible, I told myself, that something nasty could be creeping around in the unfamiliar darkness. So, basic ablutions were completed in double-quick time, although feet-washing was a wasted effort as the fetid mud claimed them immediately they touched the ground.

I remember worrying that my room was unattended. I feared for my Walkman and clothes, precious possessions at the start of a three-month stay in a land devoid of material items and with long hours to fill. I also dreaded finding my passport chewed or ripped to shreds, for how would I ever get home?

Home seemed a million miles away. Had I finally taken my adventures one step too far? All my life I'd talked the talk, but walking this particular walk felt fraught with danger. I was too anxious and exhausted to start my water filtering device, so settled for dirty teeth to match my dirty feet. I bolted the kitchen door as instructed by the cook before she went off duty.

I made my way back, carefully retracing my steps. Two small boys, dressed only in T-shirts, were peering through the keyhole to my room. They were surely a couple of moments away from entering. Thieving comes easily to those who have nothing; particularly, I've found, if you're starving, regularly beaten and unloved. I shooed them away gently and watched them scamper down the corridor. Their little bodies disappeared into the pitch of the night.

As I tried to sleep on the squalid mattress I heard children's voices somewhere in the building. And then, those screams of human terror so much nearer. There was a consistent sound of children's feet beating on stone floors; angry shouts mingled with jeering and laughter. I knew the night watchman was ensconced in his shack somewhere outside the camine but his purpose was to keep the building secure, not to look after me or the children. The children were inside, unsupervised and on the move. And I was locked inside with them.

When the screams started I could lie in my bed no longer and dressed to investigate. Shorts and a T-shirt were thrown on in the darkness and I grabbed trainers as a safe option for dirty feet. I promised myself I'd keep my back to the walls and wield my torch as a weapon if threatened. I remember being worried that the older kids, a couple of them as tall as me, might jump on my back and attack me. My hands were damp and I was shaking with fear.

What met my eyes that night is branded in my psyche. It was a tableau of horror that no one should ever witness. But, with hindsight, it was instrumental in strengthening my determination to make a difference, however small, in this decaying land. It's probably what kept me coming back over the years and it was certainly the defining moment that stopped me ever giving up, even when the quest to make a difference faded from my line of vision.

A small, deaf boy called Julian was tied to a bed. I'd been playing with him earlier in the day and I'd photographed his joy at discovering coloured balloons which he'd tossed in the air and caught with amazing dexterity. Now, his little hands were secured by thin rope and attached to the painted metal bars of the bed head. His bare backside was slightly raised above a filthy, wet mattress. His little skinny legs reached only halfway down the bed; they were held apart by two older boys who were twisting his feet at an awkward angle in order to gain purchase. His screams were heart-wrenching; his hair was soaked in sweat, his blue eyes wide with terror. I noticed he'd wet himself.

The biggest boy in the camine, a bully I'd already chastised over his treatment of the small children, was kneeling on the bed. He was raping this poor little scrap while others looked on. With pants around his ankles, the monster was doing his worst. His huge erection thrust into this little boy, each stroke raising a louder scream than the one before. And onlookers were encouraging with shouts and laughter.

Did I shout first or lunge with my torch and hit the monster on the head? I'm truly not sure. Somehow, I managed to topple the perpetrator on to the floor, much to the amusement of the other kids. I shouted for the child to be untied, my arms whirling like windmills. Strangely, my lack of Romanian vocabulary was no deterrent. The boy was released and he scarpered into the darkness like a ferret down a hole. Not before I saw blood running down his little legs.

The rapist picked himself up and shook his penis at me as some kind of greeting. He pulled his trousers up without modesty and grinned. With a shrug of indifference he slowly swaggered away with an entourage of older boys in his wake. His evil intention was thwarted for tonight, but what about tomorrow?

Strangely, all fear had left me; it was replaced by anger, so hot and uncontrolled that a revenge killing was not out of the question. Luckily, my mood cooled quickly as I recognised the scale of the situation I'd witnessed. I suspect I was suffering from shock and I remember it took over an hour for my hands to stop shaking. I stood there in the dark with my back to a stone wall and internalised the enormity of the scene. Being a realist, I knew nothing more could be achieved that night so I returned to my room. My own vulnerability was suddenly very real, too.

As I made my way back, lit only by torchlight, I met a posse of the older lads swaggering along the dank corridor. They looked menacing and puffed up and, as if by magic, large sticks appeared in their hands. Were they destined to assault me? Somewhere in my temple beat an unfamiliar pulse. A panic button was triggered; my mouth dried and lungs were slow to inflate. I hugged the wall for meagre safety and watched in horror as the assailants ignored me but started to beat any child in their path. Small children scuttled around, scared half to death. I looked into a salon and further long pieces of wood emerged from under mattresses. It was surreal. I shouted and arm-waved again, but the situation, one of systematic brutality and survival of the fittest, was played out before me. It sickened me to the core of my being.

There was no sleep for me that night. I wedged a heavy sewing-machine table under the door handle of my room and watched, hour by hour, until the pale, grey light turned to rose and gold. A new day emerged.

What I could not have known, back then, was that three of those teenage, stick-wielding boys would be become part of my extended family. I would grow to love them in a way that would surprise not only me, but my family and friends, too. Those boys were caught in a sickening life-cycle of brutality and self-preservation. And they knew no better.

The next morning I tried to find little Julian but he was nowhere to be seen. I asked one of the older girls to help me look for him but he appeared to have gone to ground. She went off to search him out while I beat a path to the director's office. It was hard to contain my fury. How could she not know what was happening in her camine? Why was there no one on duty at night to prevent such behaviour? So many questions filled my head and my anger threatened to boil over.

I was invited into the inner sanctum. Coffee was ordered although I was not in the mood for socialising. The director and I had some French vocabulary in common and I struggled to make my case. It was perfectly clear she knew what I was trying to tell her – sign language for child cruelty is much the same in any language, I suspect. She shrugged her shoulders, uninterested, and carried on with her paperwork. I was dumbstruck. This was a fast learning curve for me. These kids had no allies. This atrocity was being passed off as 'normal behaviour.'

By eleven o'clock that day I'd managed to find Julian. He'd been hiding in the pig-pen, finding solace with the animals. I found a sweet to tempt him out and gently tried to check if he was still bleeding. He was happy to be found by someone kind and allowed me to brush the straw from his little body. He had the distinct warmth and aroma of pig about him. I took him to the kitchen and asked cook for a cup of milk. Julian sat on my lap and drank it before being tempted to join some younger boys who were running around the corridors. That small boy was rapidly transferred to another camine and I never saw him again.

****

My journey had taken me to the far north-east of Romania, one of the eastern outposts of Europe. And in 1991, before the breakup of Russia, the village of Giurcani in the county of Vaslui was just three miles from the Russian border. Situated two hours south of the university city of Iasi, the village is small by any standards and could not object to being labelled a rural backwater. Many inhabitants had never been more than twenty miles from the village in their lifetimes.

One long, straight dirt road with winding, narrow pathways disappearing off at regular intervals is what meets the eye as you enter Giurcani. Single storey, rusty, tin-roofed houses are scattered as far as the eye can see. Ducks and geese waddle across the length and breadth of the village and curious, skinny children peep from behind stark metal fences and stacks of hay.

In the summertime, dust from the road swirls unmercifully around every living thing. The regular comings and goings of horses and carts lift swathes of dust into eyes and settles grit between toes. Flies torment, mosquitoes bite. When the rains come they're monsoon-like and ruthless and the entire village is a bath of thick, sticky mud. In winter the road is impassable. Mountains of snow can block the village for weeks.

The villagers, around a couple of hundred families, have lived in Giurcani for generations. They are a close-knit community and cautiously welcome the arrival of foreigners.

When I first visited, soon after Ceausescu was shot, local people sniffed the tantalising fragrance of a wealthy culture on us, the volunteers; they breathed deeply before we whipped away their dreams of a better life. We slipped in and out of their country, carefree and always able to return to our cosy lives. For them, after the anticipation of a long-awaited new life when Ceausescu fell, the dream of better things was already fading. They were resigning to a continued life of hardship and it was written all over their weary faces.

Village life was tough – tough in the sense of Wild West settlers or life for the Pilgrim Fathers. And it's still tough today. High unemployment makes it difficult for the people to provide even the basics of life for their families and leaves little enthusiasm or energy to show concern for orphans. A euphemism, of course, as most of those children in the camine weren't orphans. The reality was they were children being punished for their disabilities; punished because their parents were too poor to keep them and some were, indeed, punished when their parents were inconsiderate enough to die while they were young.

Village women who worked in the camine were indoctrinated to believe that disability must be shut away. It was considered a shame, a scar on society. They believed such children to be the responsibility of the State. As such, they were no more than a source of essential income to support their own families.

The camine nestled on the fringe of the village. When I first visited I discovered a time-warp; a vacuum of seventy or so children squeezed by communism until they gasped and choked on the corruption of those in power. And little change was seen for over a decade. It was a world apart from civilisation, as we know it. Grey lives, grey walls and grey ideals amalgamated under a disintegrating tin roof. The indifference of those who should have cared was chilling. Those kids were kept like festering bugs on a laboratory bench. There was no breath of hope within those walls and little sign of humanity.

For first-time visitors the camine was easy to find. At the far end of the village the building sat on a small incline, surrounded by wire fencing which gathered to meet a huge, metal gate. Was it keeping people in or keeping people out? I never decided. One volunteer told me that when she first arrived she took the half-sun embedded in the iron work of that gate as a positive sign. For me there was nothing inside that place that I could ever describe as 'positive'.

The Russian Orthodox Church stole the skyline behind the grim institution, suggesting that belief in God had not deserted this village, despite the forty years of struggle under Ceausescu. I was interested to find, over the years, that religion does, indeed, play a significant part in the ebb and flow of village life. Weddings, Saints' Days, Easter, Christmas, Christenings and funerals all play their part within the life-cycle of the people. And also, of course, the forgiveness of sins.

The camine building was huge by village standards with many boarded-up windows. A large part of the building was wrapped around by a glass conservatory which attracted unbearable heat in the summer and failed to hold back the biting winds of winter. The wooden doors and windows were washed with pale blue paint that had peeled with age. Attempts were made, probably years before judging by the dilapidated state of the stone-work, to create a raised, circular flower bed in front of the building. But no essence of any living thing grew from the dry, dusty soil – not that I ever saw. Everything was tired, crumpled and overdue for a face-lift which wasn't coming any time soon.

On that first visit the camine was surrounded by acres of cultivated land; waving corn, wheat ripening in the sun and fruit trees fat with promise. My curious eyes saw what looked like a small farm on the outer limits of the land. Old outbuildings, pig pens and at least one cow. A couple of dogs yapped a warning and one, I remember, had a penchant for ankles. The camine horse was tethered in the heat, fully harnessed and without an ounce of spare fat on its puny, sweating body. It was swatting big, fat flies with its tail and looked the picture of misery. But worse misery lurked inside.

The entrance to the camine was through french double doors and some older boys shepherded me towards them. I batted aside filthy net curtains at the doorway which I later learnt were to deter the profusion of flies that breed in Guircani. I could see into the dark corridor and my stomach started to flutter. And that first whiff of deprivation drifted on a faint breeze.

The floor was bare stone and under assault from a mop and bucket. A tall, sullen boy slopped copious amounts of water around and then retrieved it with his mop. He oozed it through the plastic grid into his bucket and over his plastic sandals for good measure. I remember thinking he was more man than child and wondered if he was a member of staff or one of the children.

I was met in the corridor by two enthusiastic girls. The first one wore a red tartan skirt (outgrown school uniform sent from England?) with just a ragged vest and bare feet. She limped and dragged her left leg behind her but my eyes were drawn to her beaming smile. The other, slightly older girl was naked and blood ran down her legs. She had her period but no apparent means of dealing with it. Her distended stomach reminded me of African documentaries. I knew that starvation can mislead the onlooker, creating a false impression with its fat belly and woeful eyes. My heart went out to this girl.

A scruffy, blond boy with bright blue eyes, probably aged about thirteen, urged me further inside. The boy with the mop and bucket pushed past to empty its content outside. He chucked the water against the wall of the building where it stained the dreary grey to a suspect brown before it ran in rivulets across the weather-bitten, concrete path. The smell was 'sewage special.'

As I took another couple of steps into the camine the stench of human misery choked my nostrils. The blond boy, Adrian, beckoned me to turn left along a corridor and into the dining-room, coaxing me with his light- bulb smile. Members of staff made an appearance. Women dressed in blue overalls and white headscarves with deeply wrinkled faces stared at me. It was hard to define their ages as life had clearly taken its toll. They, too, were curious and chattered among themselves, speculating, maybe, about this strange, foreign woman dressed in shorts and T- shirt.

A boy, who could have been as old as seventeen, was sweeping the refectory floor with a long-handled broom. He watched me with suspicion as he moved the long, brown, wooden benches and tables around, scraping them across the stone floor and barely taking his gaze off me. Suddenly, he decided he would sweep the floor exactly where I stood. However many times I moved out of his way he knocked my shins with the broom to make me move somewhere else. The women appeared to chastise him but to no avail. Good game for him, but it hurt. Eventually I shouted at him, in English, to stop being such a little pest. He was momentarily taken aback by the foreign onslaught and then his face broke into an enormous smile. He picked up his brush and shuffled off. And that was my first introduction to Ionelle, the oldest boy in the camine and the one to be wary of.

As I sat, with rising trepidation, on the hard wooden benches surrounded by staff and children, I noticed the dented, metal dishes and cheap, twisted spoons stacked on a shelf above the serving-hatch to the kitchen. They were decidedly grubby and well used. I wondered how seventy children were fed in this small dining-room; the answer would become apparent. They weren't. Only the strongest and able-bodied made it into the dining-room at mealtimes.

One corner of the stark room was filled with a typical Romanian stove; brown, high gloss tiles built around a chimney which covered a large proportion of the wall from ceiling to floor. Those wood-burners are a lifeline in the winter months and are replicated in all Romanian homes where they are used for both cooking and heating. The incongruous, rather grand light-fitting, which for some reason was madly off-centre, had one bulb where there should be five. There was nothing else in the room.

More children came to inspect me and the noise level slowly rose. Suddenly, with a shout and much jabbering I became aware that another boy had arrived from outside. I was reliably informed he was called Dorin. He looked about fifteen and was physically challenged. At first glance he appeared to have no hands or feet, but closer proximity showed he had a thumb on each arm where his elbow should be. He lacked the long bones in his legs and had twisted stumps instead of feet which gave him a pronounced shambling walk. But he was handsome and dynamic and clearly annoyed that he'd missed my arrival.

He scattered what I thought was a myriad of questions in my direction, clearly unable to grasp that I didn't understand a word he said. He had eyes like melting toffee which sparkled with more life than I thought could exist in such a place. Banter broke out between Dorin and the staff and I sensed he was liked by everyone. He was a breath of fresh air.

When I entered the living block proper it was taste rather than smell that further assaulted me. So thick was the stench of human excrement hanging on the warm air that the roof of my mouth dried out like a salt flat and coaxed my tongue to stick to its arid surface. A reflex action sent one hand to my nose while the other scrabbled for a handkerchief. My fixed smile slipped to somewhere around my churning stomach.

The older children, delighted with my arrival, encouraged me deeper into the dark, unwelcoming passageways. They jabbered and beckoned for me to follow them into the rooms beyond. A lad called Gheorgie took my hand to ensure I didn't make an escape. How intuitive was that boy? He had a bad attack of conjunctivitis in both eyes and I wondered if he was being treated and how many other children he'd infected.

I hadn't experienced fear since I was a child, but this place instilled it in bucket loads. Self preservation and sweaty palms told me to get out as I advanced gingerly down the corridor. But my passion to help the children gave me a good slap on the wrist. Failing at the first hurdle wasn't an option.

I walked deeper into the gloom. I remember stepping over shit which was casually deposited in the passageway. There was an eerie silence lying beyond the two excited boys who led the way. Other children and the chattering staff brought up the rear. It was hard to believe that more than seventy children were incarcerated in this place. Where were they all? How had they not died of disease? Time would reveal the answers to all my questions, but nothing would ever rinse the memory of that initial visit from my mind.

On entering one of the salons, (dormitories) I found toddlers in a blacked-out room, two to each rusting cot or bed. Slowly my eyes adjusted to the gloom and I could just make out shapes on filthy mattresses or bare wire springs. Babies vied for space with piles of excrement on the sodden sheets. There was not a whimper from any of them. Some, those able to sit, rocked gently without turning their limpid brown eyes in my direction. Interest in the world had long ago been obliterated. Skin the colour of milk covered matchstick limbs, most too weak to support their body weight. Some of them wore clothes, but everything was soiled. For the naked ones, shivers suggested cold had seeped into their little bodies, even on a warm day in May. Nothing penetrated the rooms except the smell of poverty and neglect. Neither light nor sun filtered in through boarded-up windows and I remember, particularly, those dirty, cold stone floors. I'd seen better conditions in cowsheds.

****

I was not alone in the early years. People came from far and wide to help in the camine and for a while, our progress was palpable. Gradually, we all acclimatised to the stench of communal living and the nauseous reek of human deprivation. Eventually, if we stayed long enough, we learnt to turn a blind eye to the piles and puddles of various hues and textures that lingered on the floors; sometimes they defied even the most persistent mop and bucket. But what I never quite mastered, no matter how often I returned, was to rinse the stark images of those spindly little legs; the blackened teeth and chocolate, yearning eyes. Yes, it was the eyes, mostly, that haunted my dreams; and the small hands that reached through metal bars and craved our touch.

I often think what an arrogant person I must have been when I set out on my mission, but hindsight is a wonderful thing. How could I hope to make even the slightest dent in the camine system? The government needed to change, as did people's attitudes to disability. Money was needed. Time and effort from skilled volunteers would take years to make an impact. And not least, there was a need for the Romanian people to *desire* change. The plight of Romania's children was country wide and urgent. I don't think I gave any of those issues a thought. I just waded in, heart first.

But if ignorance is bliss, then it worked for me. Over the next twenty years I coaxed hundreds of people to help me make life better for those seventy children. And also, to achieve a dream for three particular boys, Adrian, Dorin and Gheorgie, who wanted nothing more than to leave the camine and live a simple life, free from fear, hunger and deprivation. It's been an exciting voyage of discovery but with a lot of tears along the way.

Chapter 2

My story began in 1991 in the beautiful Isles of Scilly. At the time it was my much loved home amid the blue seas, white sands and lovely people. I ran a bed-and-breakfast establishment on the island of St. Mary's for several years, but eventually found it incredibly difficult to manage alone. I gave up the struggle and went in search of something new to do.

After much thought, I'd sold the business in the spring of that year and was looking forward to a few months of relaxation before taking on my next challenge. I had a small boat bobbing in the harbour and planned to be zipping around the islands, enjoying the summer with friends.

I was due to take up post as a Dame at Eton College in the autumn but I knew I would always return to that boating paradise. To that end, I purchased a small house on St. Mary's which I considered 'home'. My plan was to return to the islands during the generous school holidays I hoped to enjoy at Eton.

It was a time in my life when my two grown-up sons were settled and had no immediate need for their mum. Robert, my younger son, was living and studying in Bath and had a good network of friends. James was, well, just being James, which was very self-sufficient. The boy's dad had died when they were young and as a single mum I was independent and ready for new challenges. Little did I know what was just around the corner.

Shortly after my job offer came from Eton College, I was watching television at home one evening. I remember I'd seen a trailer about a programme called *Challenge Anneka* and was keen to watch it. The series involved the television personality Anneka Rice taking on seemingly impossible challenges and resolving them. That night's programme was filmed in a Romanian orphanage.

What many of us saw that night would reverberate around the world. I watched in horror as people saw, for the first time, the conditions within the camines. Anneka's bombshell exposure of the plight of those children was a pivotal moment in my life. It was like an itch I had to scratch and I couldn't get the images out of my mind. The sight of Anneka moved to tears was bad enough, but it was the small children with their huge eyes and skinny arms and legs that lingered. I couldn't turn my back on such cruelty and deprivation and my response to the programme was immediate. I was determined to go to Romania and help.

I had the time and the inclination which seemed enough. Having nursing experience and being mother to two boys, I felt qualified – or as qualified as anyone else was likely to be. And those were the only considerations I made, as far as I can remember.

The Anneka Rice programme was also watched by members of staff working at the Marks and Spencer store in Norwich. They, like thousands of others, felt a need to respond and set about fund-raising to help. Their intent was to take aid by lorry out to the orphanages. And that group of strangers in Norwich, through a convoluted pathway, became influential in my life and led all of us to the remote village of Giurcani.

When I contacted the *Challenge Anneka* programme-makers to express a desire to help, they explained that Southampton University had set up a database of potential volunteers and organisations working in Romania. Via this facility and a complicated web of telephone calls, I eventually made contact with Jane Clarke from the Marks and Spencer group of friends in Norwich.

Jane had spearheaded the local campaign to take aid to Romania. She and her friends were early responders and after searching maps of Romania the group agreed they would travel to the town of Baccau, which is situated in the far north-east of the country. They decided to take a lorry of aid, including clothes and toys, and eight of them set out full of hope and trepidation. In Baccau, they expected to find several orphanages and it seemed as good a place as any. However, upon arrival they discovered that many lorries had gone before them and all the camines had received aid.

The group took advice from the sisters at the Mother Teresa Home on the outskirts of the town and followed directions to the remote village of Giurcani, a camine where no foreign aid had yet arrived. This chance information led them, and eventually me, to the small Romanian village.

The friends reached their destination, tired, dusty but jubilant. Slowly, the lorry was manoeuvred over the ruts and humps of the dirt track which led to the shuttered, ugly camine building. They saw for the first time the tin roof, the cracked, concrete pathway and the ugly, low-level building sitting within acres of land. But there was a hopelessness about it that deflated their spirits, even before they reached the entrance.

Some skinny teenage boys came to meet them, shuffling down the dusty driveway. Despite ragged clothes, broken shoes and spotty faces, their beaming welcome entranced the visitors. Jane jumped down from the lorry to say hello and was met with an excitement that was palpable. Visitors were rare at the camine, particularly such strange-looking ones.

****

For any Western visitors to the camine in Giurcani in the 1990s, it was a surreal experience. The Anneka Rice programme had prepared people in a small way, but the reality was so much worse. Room after stinking room of human horror met the eye. Scabby children lay in cots and beds, most of them untouched by human hand. The beds and cots were packed together like sardines and the pale faces of the tiny inhabitants wrenched at heartstrings. The dark, shuttered rooms with stark stone floors and no glass in the boarded-up windows chilled the soul. And there was no sound. No laughter, no cries – just an eerie silence. Urine ran on the floors and the stench caused bile to rise in onlookers' throats.

There was a distinct division of children. The older, apparently healthy, although skinny and under-developed ones who worked outside on the land; the smaller mobile children who never went outside and the sickly, desperately undernourished of all ages who lingered in cots and beds, many tied down with strips of sheeting.

It was those younger children who were too weak to leave their beds who caught the immediate attention of visitors. They were a tangle of thin arms and legs, gaunt faces with eyes full of resignation, reminiscent of images of the Holocaust. Children of six or seven years old had never been fed with anything but bottles of milk. They lay like babies, unmoving and with eyes that stared constantly into space.

But the children who were mobile and able to run around the dark corridors gathered joyfully around visitors, clamouring to be picked up. They quickly learned that visitors usually meant the distribution of sweets.

All the children in the camine had physical or mental disabilities and many had weeping sores, impetigo, which was roughly daubed with gentian violet, and an array of bruises and cuts, obtained, one assumed from the unfettered violence.

I learnt that very few ills or ailments were ever treated. Boils were left to their own devices, bursting their yellow, putrid content at will with no means of dressing the wound. Toothache was rarely mentioned. It was part and parcel of the regime of neglect and must be borne until the pain prevented the child from eating or working. Then, and only then, would expense be spared to take the child to the dentist; no money was available for an anaesthetic, whatever treatment was needed.

Windows in the salons were never opened to let the rooms inhale fresh air and the children breathed nothing but the toxic stink of ammonia and faeces. The smell throughout the entire building was a living thing that crept along the floors, working its way into every nook and cranny. Instead of fresh air and freedom these children endured incarceration, starvation and deprivation of the worst kind: no touch, no kindness, no one to trust and no one to protect them. They were deprived of everything a child needs to grow and flourish. And the greatest shock of all for visitors – the staff appeared to think camine life was normal.

****

The Director for the Protection of Children in the area wanted to meet the Marks and Spencer group. He announced he'd bring a young student of English from Vaslui who would act as interpreter. The group were optimistic they could forge relationships with him as they were desperate to alleviate the squalor and create a better life for those pathetic children.

It had been agreed by the group that the aid brought from England would be distributed between the camine and the local schoolchildren. Sharing aid around the village was an ethos I also, later adopted and I believe it helped me forge friendships with village people. It did, in the main, prevent the well-documented jealousy which sprang up in many towns and villages and which led to theft and bad press.

By chance, as they left the camine, the group were flagged down by two men walking along the road. Through the cab window they discovered that these were both teachers at the local primary school. But even better, they offered accommodation to everyone for the night. This was the beginning of a friendship with Didi Rotaru, the primary school head teacher, which would be enjoyed by many volunteers who followed. On more than one occasion Didi and his wife Tori would be a refuge for me during the years ahead.

It transpired that he was an educated man with a good grasp of French, but more importantly, a deep concern for children and genuine kindness for his fellow man. Tall and slim with greying hair, he was dressed in a suit and tie, bearing little resemblance to the average villager. He had a ready smile and was clearly keen to engage with foreigners.

Books, crayons and pens were distributed for the village children and the school was opened up to receive the gifts, although lessons were over for the day. An invitation was issued for the group to look around the classrooms and to this day they still talk about the impressive array of artwork on the classroom walls. Flowers and animals, bright blue skies and smiling children were displayed like wallpaper. Hidden gems within the grim reality of Romanian life. As I got to know Didi better, I discovered he was a man who deserved to be born to more opportunities in life.

The Marks and Spencer group's first night in Giurcani turned out to be a huge success. Didi, his wife Tori, together with brother Nellu and his family welcomed and entertained the group of eight. A meal was created for them and makeshift beds found so that all had somewhere to sleep. It was a typical act of generosity from that family.

The finer points of playing Ibbly Dibbly (don't ask) were explained and shrieks of laughter echoed around the dark stillness of the village that night. The group were introduced to the outside loo (a hole in the ground inside a wooden shed), the washing facilities (a plastic tank of rain water with a tap, set up in the garden) and the constant barking of the guard dogs throughout the night. Slowly, sleep came as they lay safely tucked up in bed, in an alien land.

The next day they returned to the camine to meet with the senior Director from Vaslui. He had the dubious responsibility for all the camines in the county. A terse, towering hunk of a man under a thatch of black hair, he showed little emotion or surprise at their interest in helping. His translator was a jolly student called Radu who was thrilled to meet English people for the first time. He also acted as chauffeur to the important man.

Much discussion took place and it was agreed that volunteers could be sent out from England to work with the children. The possibility of building a wing to alleviate the overcrowding was also met with a positive response – and why wouldn't it be? It was apparent that much needed to be done to help seventy, desperate children. The group explained they wanted to make changes. Some would be immediate but others would take years of hard work and determination to achieve. And not all the children would be alive to see them. As with all volunteers that I ever met, the group never considered failure.

The Marks and Spencer friends took their leave of the village with a promise to return with more aid. In particular, they would provide new cots and beds for the children and send volunteers to help in a practical way. So, on a cloud of hope they returned home to raise more money and keep their promises.

Jane Clarke approached the head office of Marks and Spencer for a donation to help with their plans. The management was receptive to the charitable aims of their staff and promised to match-fund all money raised. And via the database to match people with organisations at Southampton University, they found me.

****

Back in beautiful Scilly, my head was still full of the images Anneka Rice brought to us of undersized, sick children rocking in rusty cots. I'd like to say I made an informed decision to go to Romania, but the truth was, I didn't even look at an atlas or research anything about the country or its politics.

Little had been documented about Romania for many years. To all intents and purposes it had been a closed country under the dictator, Ceausescu. We, in the west knew little about the forty years of his tyrannical rule as he'd managed to keep his atrocities under wraps, in line with other dictators around the world. Consequently, a country of cowed, angry people festered, right under his nose. Eventually, on Christmas Day in 1989, the boil burst and the people turned on him and his wife with a gun.

I was fortunate to have three months to spare before starting my new job at Eton College so what could be simpler than a humanitarian trip to a country no one seemed to know much about? Could I achieve anything

27

worthwhile in that time? I had to try. Crying about television images was an understandable, immediate response, but not a helpful one. Not for those poor kids, anyhow.

Long conversations with Jane Clarke filled in details and it took very little to get me hooked. Just to hear the emotion in her voice as she told me of her experiences was enough. I knew I had to go and in my head I was already packing a rucksack. She explained I had to pay my own airfare but promised to arrange for me to be met at Bucharest airport and taken to the village by an English-speaking Romanian. He had family living in Giurcani and would stay with them for a few days to help settle me in. Upon arrival I would also be offered hospitality 'for a day or two' with his aunt and her family.

Jane told me she'd left a supply of tinned food in the village in readiness for any volunteers that might follow but she could not guarantee it would still be there. She also thought there was a chance I would be joined by someone else who had expressed an interest in going to Giurcani.

The other person who was prepared to venture into the unknown was a lady called Angela Cowles who lived in Maidstone. She had also responded to the Anneka programme and was probably going to join me. And indeed, that is how it turned out. Angela and I would face many of the early challenges together.

In Norwich money was rolling in to get the building project underway. Jane and the group were working hard and it looked as if the extension to the camine would definitely go ahead. Marks and Spencer Head Office agreed to send a surveyor to carry out the preliminary work and it was likely to happen while I was living in the village. That sounded like a safety net to me, albeit a small one.

****

I left Scilly on April 27th 1991 and spent a couple of days with close friends, Annie and Peter Carter in Bristol. Annie and I have been friends since our nursing days and we are godparents to each other's children.

As I still needed to shop for a few bits and pieces, we went to the shopping centre in Broadmead where I purchased a plate, bowl and mug – a jolly melamine set festooned with colourful parrots. It was much admired by camine children for many years. I also stocked up on slide film, (how old fashioned that now seems) and a few treats for the children. But it was from Temple Meads Station that the real journey began on May 1st.

I had stuffed everything I thought I might need in a new, bright green rucksack. Three months seemed a long time to manage if I forgot any essentials so I tried to think of everything. I knew nothing would be available to buy once I arrived.

I'd made a list and it included:

Sleeping bag (new, lightweight and very small when packed into its own little bag)

Books

Walkman and tapes

Writing paper and pens

Diary

2 pairs of shorts

4 T-shirts

6 pants
2 bras
2 pairs of socks
Tracksuit bottoms
2 pairs of jeans
Sweatshirt
Sandals
Trainers
Liquid washing soap for clothes
Sterile needles and syringes (in case of emergencies)
Water filter system (expensive, but easy to use)
Plate, bowl, knife, fork, spoon
Antibiotics (one basic course from friendly GP)
Laxatives
Suncream
Bonjela
Anti-histamine
Disposable gloves
Nail scissors

All of the above, plus a few gifts for the children, which consisted of crayons, chewing gum, biros and drawing paper filled my rucksack to capacity. It appeared I hadn't grasped the fact when I bought it that 'large rucksack' can equal 'heavy'. When I had a trial run at Annie's, I found it was almost impossible to heave the fully packed bag onto my back. I'd never been a Girl Guide and never camped so I was something of a virgin where rucksacks were concerned.

But the die was cast and somehow, I knew I would manage. I'd acquired a quantity of American dollars which, I was assured, was the currency of choice. (I think I exchanged about five hundred pounds.) I bought a substantial bum-bag to hold things such as passport and money, and so it was that the adventure began.

When Annie and Peter saw me off at Temple Meads I told them about a dream I'd had the previous night. I dreamt I'd fallen over on a dusty, foreign road due to the weight of my rucksack and I was stranded on my back like a beetle. No amount of kicking of arms and legs could get me back on my feet. Hot sun beat down and shrivelled me up to nothing. Hmm . . . more like a nightmare. And with that happy thought and much giggling and hugs from Annie, I was on my way.

When I reached Heathrow I was early for the agreed meeting with Angela. I hung around the shopping mall, afraid to take the rucksack off my back for fear I would never get it on again. I was already feeling the excess weight on my spine. Oh dear! I tried to lean nonchalantly around the shops, taking some weight off my shoulders. I'm sure I looked as if I was casing the joint.

I eventually met up with Angela who was likewise laden and we sat for a while with her family who had come to see her off. I thought about my two sons and hoped that they would be OK. They were both adults but what difference does that make to a mother? I knew that communication would be almost impossible from the village and had arranged for my friend Debs in Scilly to stay in touch with them. I also had my beloved Aunt Pat on alert. I knew she loved my boys and also, I knew I'd raised two sensible, independent lads. Nevertheless, I couldn't help worrying.

After Angela said goodbye to her family and we'd passed through passport control we were met by a friend called Gordon Tilsley. He was, at that time, a photographer making his living at Heathrow airport where he photographed the rich and famous as they passed through the terminals. He was a regular holidaymaker in Scilly where we'd shared many a pint of beer in the Mermaid pub.

Gordon had kindly offered to meet us and take us to the VIP lounge for refreshments. Here, we had delicious nibbles and a glass or two of champagne in luxury usually assigned to first class passengers. We relaxed and had a chance to take our minds off the task ahead. But we came close to missing our flight. Gordon told us he would keep an eye on the departure board but, when I queried if it was time for us to board, he confessed he thought we were going to Budapest. We made it in time and it was a lovely send-off. By the time we boarded Tarom airlines to Bucharest we were both feeling relaxed.

The flight to Romania was an event in itself. As a fairly seasoned traveller I had basic expectations about standards on aircraft, many of which went out of the cabin window within the first ten minutes.

The first shock was the overhead lockers, or should I say, shelves. They had no closure over the contents and reminded me of luggage racks on buses when I was a kid. I'd bought myself a bottle of Baileys in Duty Free and was concerned that it should remain safe on the luggage rack and particularly, that it didn't fly off and hurt someone.

When I mentioned my concerns to one of the cabin crew she glowered at me and said, 'Put on floor. Under seat.' Well, that told me.

The stewardesses kept us amused. A smile or gesture of politeness was out of the question, it seemed. Three, grim-faced, middle-aged women patrolled the aisles, looking at the travellers as if they were criminals. They wore thick makeup which was applied with little finesse and stark navy uniforms which gave more than a nod to prison guards. We made up rude names for them. Yes, our behaviour was on a par with school kids and probably due, in no small part, to the glasses of bubbly we'd enjoyed.

There was a group of Saga members on board and I remember being impressed that they had chosen Romania for their holiday. At that time the land of Dracula was definitely not a usual tourist destination. There were also a number of Romanians travelling home. They were easy to spot by their poor quality, unfashionable clothes, their high volume of chatter and the general air of excitement they exuded at the thought of takeoff. I liked them. They seemed a jolly sort of people and I was looking forward to meeting some.

There was an hour's delay out on the tarmac because of oil on the wheels of the aircraft and the cabin heated up quickly amid cries for air conditioning to be turned on. Apparently, this was not possible in a stationary aircraft so we quietly sweated in our seats.

We were unable to see what method was used to combat the problem but eventually the aircraft took off. There were rather disconcerting rattles reverberating around the now silent passengers. I thought the noise came from the wings but Angela thought it might be a fault in the engine. Neither was a comforting scenario. There was a general hubbub of noise with much clapping from the excitable Romanians as we became airborne and I decided they were going to be fun people to live amongst.

The food on board is probably best unremarked upon, but suffice to say, Angela and I agreed we had probably eaten our last decent food for some time to come. The champagne and nibbles already seemed a distant memory.

During the flight we spent time getting to know one another. We compared expectations, exchanged medical details – I must be sure never to put Elastoplasts on Angela's skin as she is allergic – and we had a fit of the giggles when I confessed, in the best traditions of safety, I had packed condoms! It looked as if we would get along.

****

We were met at Otopeni Airport, as promised, by an English-speaking Romanian called Renato. Angela and I were concerned about the delay at Heathrow and hoped he had waited for us. We dared not think of the consequences if he wasn't there.

But before we reached the meet and greet area we had to forge our way through the baggage collection and the visa department. And I had never seen such chaos. Hundreds of excitable people were milling around, pushing and shoving and talking in high, excited voices. We didn't think about it at the time, but for most Romanians it would have been the first time they had travelled abroad.

The fabric of the airport was antiquated and dirty. Windows high up in the corrugated roof space were grimed with green-tinged dirt; the floors were grubby with litter and the whole area had the charm of a concentration camp. (They now have a modern, glass building which compares with any European terminal.) But most alarming for me was the staff. Not only were they grim-faced, uniformed and lurking around every corner, but they were equipped with large guns and looked more than capable of using them. No one smiled as we took our place in a long queue to collect our luggage. I was secretly afraid we would have no luggage to collect or, at the very least, it would have been pilfered.

After an age our rucksacks appeared, sandwiched between black bin liners of stuff, parcels tied with string and antiquated suitcases which appeared to be the more normal type of luggage. My relief was considerable as I retrieved my worldly goods from the conveyor belt and heaved them into position. There was definitely a knack to this rucksack business, I decided, and I was slowly getting the hang of it.

Now we had to queue again to get our visas which cost us the exorbitant price of fifty dollars each. I remember feeling grumpy that we had come to offer aid to the country but had to pay such a huge amount for the pleasure of an entry visa. I would get used to it over the coming years, but it always felt unfair. Eventually, of course, when Romania joined the EU, everyone from Europe was able to enter without a visa. However, I always felt that staff working at the airport or border agencies felt cheated by the new simplicity. Officialdom is inbred in Romanians – nurtured, of course, by the rule of Ceausescu. Many times I have been heard to mutter about awarding a 'jobsworth cap' to surly government workers who would rather impede your progress than help. Happily, those people are getting fewer and are more than compensated for by the lovely, warm Romanians who have offered me kindness.

Some two and a half hours late we emerged from the baggage hall with not only our luggage and a visa, but also a small amount of lei acquired at a currency exchange. Again we queued but gradually got the hang of the Romanian method of elbowing aside anyone standing in front of you. This moved things along a little quicker and caused Angela and I some amusement. We developed a 'when in Rome' attitude to life remarkably quickly.

The currency exchange would only take American dollars, for which we were prepared. The exchange rate in 1991 was 325 lei to the dollar. We were millionaires!

Renato held up a placard with our names on – I've always held a childish desire to be met in this manner – and after introductions, this short, Latin-looking young man with a ponytail made his way to the airport exit. We followed.

The terminal was mayhem. The most noticeable thing for me was the walnut-skinned gypsies. They thronged around in bunches of eight or ten, mostly women and some with papoose style attachments from which small, black-haired babies poked their heads. The women were unsmiling and looked on with black, searching eyes. They wore amazing long, multi-coloured skirts which swished around their ankles and gathered at the waist.

Tight bodices, laced at the front, flaunted an ample supply of bosom.

Renato told us to hold on to our valuables as theft was commonplace and the women were, he explained, experts. I thought of Fagin from the musical *Oliver* and found myself watching to see if I could witness the act of theft before my eyes. I couldn't. They drifted around in groups, eyeing the crowds and presumably looking for someone careless with their belongings. What an exciting prospect we must have been.

Angela and I followed Renato like lambs to the slaughter, rarely taking our eyes off him for fear of being lost in such a hostile environment. Of course, over the years these scenes have become the norm.

When we eventually got outside the evening heat hit us like a blanket of fire. And even more chaos danced around, mostly in the form of vociferous taxi drivers touting for fares, gypsy men smoking and drinking bottles of beer and everyday working people going about their business. There was the general milling of travellers, as seen in any capital city in the world, but it was the poverty around us that was impossible to ignore. Tatty clothes, children without shoes and cars which looked as if they had come on board the Ark, all spoke of deprivation. There was also a heavy pollution in the air which created a hazy sunshine, despite the searing heat.

Angela and I must have had eyes coming out on stalks. Renato explained, in reasonable English, that his family were waiting to meet us as they had never seen a foreign person. As if by magic, his father and younger brother appeared with big smiles and outstretched hands. They were clearly curious about two western women who were lugging their worldly goods around in rucksacks. Over the next few days we noticed how much we stood out from the crowd. We bore no resemblance to local women.

Renato told us it was too late to travel on to Giurcani that day but he'd arranged for us to stay in Bucharest with his cousins. After we said our goodbyes to his charming family we took a taxi from the queue of eager taxi drivers. Our luggage was stowed in the boot and we squeezed into an old Dacia car which coughed and spluttered its way out of the airport concourse. We craned our necks to take a first glimpse of the city which looked very 'Iron Curtain' and exciting.

Renato suggested that we would travel via Ceausescu's Palace which was clearly a building of much renown. Even we from the western world were astounded by the size and grandeur of it – 'twenty-six football pitches long', we were proudly informed. How could a man live with such wealth yet allow Romania's people to live in abject poverty? The opulence of the palace was legendary among the people. No wonder they shot him.

Renato's cousin turned out to be a charming man with two adult daughters called Dorothea and Nina. They lived in a clean, welcoming apartment high above the city in a typical brick, high-rise building. It was an ugly tenement block and first impression told us it was identical to dozens of others we'd seen around the city. It reminded me of slum communities I'd seen in Glasgow in the sixties which were demolished years ago.

To reach our accommodation we had to climb eight flights of concrete stairs as a hand-written notice attached to the lift announced it was waiting for repair. There were few lights so we trudged ever upwards in semi-darkness. When asked about the lack of illumination Renato was unsure if the light bulbs were broken or the electricity was switched off – either way we had to watch our footing on the crumbling, concrete steps. The ascent was taxing due to the weight we were both carrying. I remember that at the grand age of forty-four I could definitely feel the strain. But I took heart, for the next day it would be all downhill.

When we arrived at the apartment we were welcomed into a sparsely furnished home of which the cousins were clearly proud. Nina spoke a little English and was fascinated to know about our lives. Did we really all have a colour television? Did we all have jobs and plenty to eat? Did we go to the coast for our holidays? Dorothea was shy and spoke very little but she was interested in everything that was being said and translated for her by Renato.

We had a supper of boiled eggs, hard cheese, bread and coffee. The apartment boasted an indoor bathroom complete with flushing loo where we washed and changed into pyjamas. We fell, exhausted into a double bed and Angela and I exchanged a look which said, 'I don't make a habit of sleeping with women I hardly know,' then we giggled and duly fell into a fitful sleep. The following day we had more eggs and bread and used the bathroom again. Little did we realise this would be the last running water we'd see for some time.

We made our way to the railway station by local bus accompanied by Dorothea and Nina. Renato suggested we exchange more dollars into lei as there would be no means to do so in the village. He then said he needed to queue to get first-class tickets at the station office, commenting that he hoped we wouldn't be introduced to second-class train travel for such a long journey. We had no idea what he meant. Second-class travel had always been good enough at home.

Paying for the tickets was our first battle with lei, the value of which has always remained a mystery to me. We pushed a wad of 'Monopoly' money into his hand as he explained that not all trains had first-class carriages but he was hopeful we would be lucky. We were in luck and he returned triumphant as, for a small pittance (to us,) Renato had purchased first class tickets to Birlad for our seven-hour journey. After that, he explained, we would need a pre-arranged car-ride to the village, which would take another hour.

We asked Renato how many lei would be an appropriate thank you to our hosts and duly paid Nina and Dorothea for our accommodation and food. We said our goodbyes and thanked the first Romanian family of our acquaintance. Chocolate had been left for them by our bedside and I hoped we'd see them again one day, although we never did.

It was then time to join the throng of people who were bustling to catch their trains. We struggled to climb aboard via particularly high, wide, metal steps. I needed a helping hand from Renato to heave the rucksack on to the train. And at precisely ten-thirty, not a minute early and not a minute late, the train left the station with much whistle-blowing, waving and shouting from a uniformed guard, resplendent in peaked cap and navy and scarlet tunic. We had our noses glued to the window to take in all the sights.

From the very comfortable, plush seats in the first-class carriage we witnessed a scene that resembled a film-set in wealthy Russia at the turn of the nineteenth century. There were people everywhere. Porters in uniform with luggage piled on carts; mothers pulling small children along and the screech of traditional Romanian music bellowing from loudspeakers and assaulting the ears. The smell of burnt diesel oil and hot metal filled our nostrils. Children munched popcorn, a cheap snack in Romania where vast amounts of corn grew at that time, as they wandered after anxious family members who urged them to keep up. And colourful gypsies were scattered like jewels across the grey, concrete station. All very strange.

And so the tedious, seven-hour journey began. We loved the comfort, the large windows and safe luggage racks above our heads which gave us confidence for the journey. I slept a little, stretched my legs in the corridors and even went for an amble into the second-class carriages.

And how pleased I was not to be ensconced in one of those. The seats were bare wood with high backs and were graced by an incongruous array of people. Many seats were shared with livestock; two ducks in a cage made a fearful noise; I also saw several chickens held in laps, a ferocious cockerel and two lambs wrapped in a blanket, bleating piteously.

The travellers were as interested in me as I was in them. I appeared to cause consternation – a middle-aged woman travelling in jeans and T-shirt which had Queen's Rock Tour logo on it. When I mentioned to Renato that I had caused some stares, he laughed and told me, 'You had better get used to it.' He warned me with a smile, 'Villagers will be fascinated by you; they'll want to know how old you are, where is your husband and why don't you wear a skirt and headscarf?' Hmm . . .

Chapter 3

We survived the journey despite the heat, the persistent, sullen gypsy women selling black sunflower seeds for snacking on and the agonising slowness of the train. I even survived the lavatory which consisted of a cubicle wherein I found a hole exposing the scary, moving train track. The entire floor was covered in excrement. I was the brave one who tried it first but after my description of the experience Angela decided she would rather keep her legs crossed, thank you. At that point she stopped drinking water to prevent the need to visit the 'facility'.

We lingered at dozens of small stations, each consisting of a concrete slab of platform on which a small hut served as the ticket office. There was much coming and going at each stop. Travellers jumped off and filled plastic bottles with water from grubby fountains before boarding again, just as the whistle-blowing guard sent us on our way. Shouts, salutations and laughter floated on the air as people alighted to make their way home.

When the train stopped in a rush of steam in Birlad a demented little man charged up and down the train, blowing his whistle and urging those who were leaving to hurry along. And, somewhat shockingly, we had to alight straight on to railway lines. Having a train stop where there was no platform, according to Renato, was not unusual and he assured us the tracks were not 'live'. So it wasn't all bad news. We needed to cross two more lines in order to reach the station platform. Very scary but no distant locomotive could be heard bearing down on us from either direction.

Although we'd arrived at Birlad, a town close to the Russian border, we still had another hour of travel eastwards before reaching Giurcani. Miraculously, the promised man with a car introduced himself, (how easy we must have been to identify) and we were whisked away through the teaming streets in a battered Dacia car. Giurcani - are you ready for us?

****

Romania is a vast country. It's an amalgam of immediate desire to change into a modern European country but hampered by historic, grinding deprivation and blinkered people in power. Judged harshly by many for her documented 'orphanage sins', the people are warm and the areas of rural landscape are breathtakingly beautiful.

Travellers can enjoy bustling cities and quiet backwaters and most are surprised by the vastness of the terrain. It's true, Romania is a little rough around the edges, but from the soft folds of her pastureland, the swell of the mighty Danube to the monasteries of the Carpathian Mountains, she's my kind of country and worthy of more visitors.

Juxtaposed around the ruthless camines, Romania's towns and cities conceal stunning architecture, albeit a little jaded. The grand, intricate buildings were created from her former wealth by clever, educated people. In the nineteen-twenties and thirties Bucharest was known as 'little Paris'. Here, royalty were entertained and her inhabitants were welcomed into the highest echelons of the world's society. Ornate, gilded opera houses can be found in comparatively small towns and bear witness to a glorious past. But not so glorious, of course, is her more recent history. Millstones of neglect hung around little necks within grey, communist camines are nothing to be proud of. And the people, stalwart and patient, so near to starvation.

Swathes of organic countryside blaze with wild flowers in springtime. The mouths of Romania's rivers yield a banquet to visiting birds amid their wetlands and marshes. An indolent summer heat burns flowers and foliage to a crisp and creates a palette of gold and burnt sienna across the land.

But my favourite season is the winter, when deep snow softens the frayed edges of heartlands and forests into an undulating, giant pillow. In the cities, mounds of white grubbiness pile high against crumbling buildings and the slush and snow halt footsteps and chill bones. The snow resists all efforts with brush and shovel; winters in Romania follow a relentless pattern. Snow will surely fall again tomorrow.

As the last century flipped a page, Romania was still dragging the baggage of Communism behind her. Experience taught her much; suspicion of foreigners, acceptance of what couldn't be changed and, importantly, thrift. The bad old days are not forgotten for who knows when another dictator could make their lives a living hell?

This is a country that would love to snip loose the label of the 'orphanage scandal', but I suspect it will be many decades before she's rewarded. To be fair, Romania has not yet fully cleaned up her act. In my view, it will take several generations and a huge desire from her people to forge change and attempt to compensate her lost children.

I stumbled across this fascinating country not by accident, but certainly not by design, either. I was on a quest to help deprived children and to seek justice for those unable to speak out, although not in a gung-ho manner. There was no fire and brimstone emanating from my lungs, that I remember. But the experience turned into so much more than the sum of its parts. On reflection, I nearly bit off more than I could chew. But for those with a belief in fate, Romania was definitely written in my stars. And after twenty-plus years of loyalty to her, I've been told I'm an 'honorary Romanian'. And I'm proud to be one.

****

Hundreds of people from all over Europe beat a path to Romania's door. Some arrived in Giurcani and most, like me, had no idea what to expect upon arrival. And there was much to be scared of if the newspapers were to be believed. Talk was rife that HIV lurked in every camine. Its cause, reportedly, was the cheap African blood given to the abandoned children while Ceausescu used their own blood in his quest to stay ever-youthful. I've never proved or disproved that story. But there were other issues for volunteers too. No one knew if the water in the village of Giurcani was safe to drink or if bottled water could be purchased. And no one even knew if the natives were friendly.

Looking back, I have no idea how I thought I was going to survive, without a support network. I learnt, much later, that registered charities have a very different approach to sending volunteers abroad and, at the very least, they are given training, food and support while they are working. Accommodation of a reasonable standard is arranged for them.

I knew not to expect a public telephone or reliable postal service in the village, to say nothing about a food source. And of course, there was also the small matter of communication as I couldn't speak the language. I had some basic French which would prove invaluable, but not a lot else was looking positive.

With hindsight, I suppose you could say I 'did it my way'. Instead of food parcels and support from people at home, I made do with whatever I could carry and, importantly, huge amounts of optimism. I believe Angela would subscribe to that view, too. More than once we asked ourselves, 'What are we doing here?' Some days we seemed a very long way from home.

Maybe there's something about your early forties that defines the DNA of your life. I was old enough to trust my instincts, young enough to think I was indestructible and freed from the responsibility of young children. Sounds like heaven. I did, however, take the precaution of stuffing surgical gloves into my rucksack in case the HIV rumours were true. I bought, at great expense, a water filtering system. And that was about it.

I decided early on that I would keep a diary of my visit. Little did I know that the diary would continue for over twenty years. Some nights, I remember, I felt exhausted and could hardly keep my eyes open to write even a sentence. But I always pushed myself to do it. And photographs – well they amount to thousands. I took slides in the early years, film and digital photos later and I treasure them all.

****

Adrian

I don't remember when Rita first arrived in our village. I can remember lots of things arriving like clothes and toys, so I guess it was around then when she and Angela first came to visit. We had loads of English people come to the village. They visited on and off for a couple of years. They all brought us stuff but none of them stayed for long. Only Rita kept coming.

I don't really like women much. I find they always want me to do something for them and they scream at me and call me stupid. But not Rita. I'd never hurt or upset her and I'd do anything to make her pleased with me. I used to dream that she was my mother when I was younger, but I don't dream that any more. She's the best thing that ever happened to me.

She and Angela liked me and used to play games and teach me songs in English. I used to sing Romanian folk songs to them that I'd learned by hanging around village weddings. Rita said I had a voice like an angel but I don't know what angels sound like so I can't say whether it was true or not. She was always saying, 'Sing, Adrian, sing'. I always want to please her so I'd sing any time she asked.

The first time she came, when I was just a kid, she hung around with us older boys a lot. For the first year or so she visited with Angela and then after that she started coming on her own. One year I was told she'd got married and I remember being worried in case her new husband didn't like us and stopped her coming to Romania. But lucky for us that didn't happen. Eric likes us too.

I was afraid of the staff at the camine. They beat me so often for not doing what they asked even though I tried my best. I'm what people call 'slow'. I don't always understand what people want and I don't remember things either. I have fits sometimes. I'm supposed to have tablets but back in the camine, they often ran out of them and I didn't have any for months. My fits got worse and then I had to have the doctor to look at me. When the doctor came to check me the director used to say she had run out of my tablets. One of the women told me they were sold to people in the village, but I don't know if that's true.

****

Dorin

I once heard someone say, 'If God wanted us to travel at the speed of light he'd have stuck a jet-propelled motor up our asses!' I suppose if He'd wanted me to have parents or proper legs He'd have sorted that, too. But He didn't, and I was left in the camine system as a kid. And a good chunk of my life as a grown-up, too. Not that I'm moaning about it. I learnt at a young age that you have to get on with whatever life throws at you and hope it gets better.

But back when I was young, I just wanted enough food to eat and some shoes that would fit my cranky feet. Well, they're not feet, really. Just stumps. Rita says my cranky bits remind her of some kids born in England, years ago. Apparently, it was to do with a drug the mothers took which resulted in babies being born without arms and legs. I

49

don't know what my mother took, or if she took anything at all, but I've got no proper hands or feet. I have two fingers that stick out from where my elbows should be and they work just fine. My legs are short, too, with twisted lumps of flesh where other people have feet. Some people call me a midget, but I'm not. I've seen midgets on television and they have funny faces. But I'm good-looking. I've got dark brown eyes that Rita tells me have a twinkle, and I've got good hair and good teeth as well. I think that kind of balances out the bad bits, don't you? The first time I saw a photo of my face (I can't remember when it was, but I was grown-up) I remember thinking, 'I'm quite a handsome man.' And then I remembered my hands and feet, or lack of them.

At some point I realised that my dream of having a wife and settling down with a couple of kids was never going to happen. But that's life and it's no use hankering after things you can't have, is it?

There was a girl in the village I was really keen on when I was younger. She told me I had beautiful brown eyes and I thought that meant she fancied me. But it didn't. When I asked if she'd like to go for a walk to the river she screamed at me. 'With a freak like you?' she bellowed, so that half the village heard. I wanted to die of embarrassment. The village men teased me about it for years. I've never dared ask a girl to go anywhere with me since. And now that girl's married with three kids. And guess what? She's not pretty any more – but I'm still good looking.

Nothing stops me doing anything I want, except I can't walk in deep snow. I sink - just like a cartoon character I sometimes watch on television. I find myself up to my neck in frozen ice and I have to be rescued. When I was a kid I couldn't go outside in the winter in case I got lost in a snowdrift.

Rita told me years ago that I could achieve anything if I really set my heart on it. I thought to myself that day, 'I'll have a house of my own in the village, please'. I didn't tell her, but it set me dreaming about what could be possible if I tried hard enough.

Life in the camine wasn't as bad as you might think. I had good mates, Adrian, Gheorgie and Dan, and we did have a laugh, sometimes. And at least we could go outside the camine building and into the village, unlike most of the kids who were tied to their beds or locked in dark, stinking rooms. So that was lucky, for a start. But we had to work hard, sometimes ten or eleven hours a day. And that was tough for kids, especially when you don't get enough to eat. Someone told me that your body adapts to having too little food and you still manage to work. Well, I'm living proof, aren't I?

It was not long after the Romanian people shot Ceausescu that I learnt how lucky I really was. And it wasn't 'cos the dictator was dead either. He never bothered me when he was alive so I wasn't bothered when they shot him. No – being lucky started one hot, sunny day, years and years ago. It was when Rita appeared in the village to work at the camine and I found out she really liked me. She was the first person who ever liked me. I didn't know it at the time, but she was going to change my life forever.

I know it was summer when she came 'cos the crops were high in the fields and flies were hugging the cow dung, *the ones that always look as if they're having a feast and can't get enough shit in their greedy mouths. (See – there's always someone with a worse life than you.)*

This particular lucky day, I remember, was a day when the flies were being a menace and if you weren't careful they'd give you a nasty bite. The dust from the land caught on the breeze and managed to get in your eyes and mouth, as if it owned you. It was the time of day when the camine staff sat outside taking a rest from the grime and smell of the rooms they worked in. They had a bucket of water and they dipped a metal cup in and passed it around the group. Sometimes they'd offer us kids a drink, but I don't think they did that day.

They were laughing at a couple of foreigners who'd arrived a few days earlier to work in the camine. It was Rita and Angela. They'd started doing stuff in the little kids' salons and persuaded the director to let them bring the children outside to get some fresh air. They were sitting on rugs on the concrete pathway and they'd given the kids bowls of water to play with.

I must admit, the English women were dressed in funny clothes and they jabbered to each other in some queer language none of us understood. The camine women thought Rita should know better than to wear shorts. She was far too old for that, they said. But I thought she looked nice. Both of them looked fresh and clean and kind and I was curious to know more about them. They definitely came from a country that was better than ours. They probably had lives like princesses with servants to bring them everything they needed, I thought.

Nicu, the groundsman looked at them full of hate. Or was it envy? He hated everybody and that included us kids. 'Why would those stupid women want to waste money and energy on mad kids?' he wanted to know, flapping his hand to find some breeze. 'You're all crazy.' He glared straight at me like I was mud under his shoe. 'You're all a waste of space.' He was smoking a thin rollup, I remember and he coughed, sniffed loudly and spat brown gunge into the dust. He lit his ciggy from a match which he struck on the sole of his shoe. 'Pity Ceausescu didn't do away with you and have done with it', he muttered to no one in particular, but I knew he meant me.

Now I was never afraid of anything until then. I felt goose-bumps prickle my arms and a real fear crept into my head. I've never forgotten it. Even though it was a hot day, I went cold just thinking about what he'd said. I'd never liked Nicu, he'd given me too many beatings for that, but after I realised how much he hated us kids I knew he was a real threat. I could be smothered while I slept or taken away and drowned like a puppy. I've seen kittens and puppies drowned in the river, loads of times. No one would have known what happened to me, and no one would have cared, either. But years have gone by. And he's dead, which is what he deserved, and I'm still here. Ha!

I remember that day for two reasons. Not just because I learnt to fear Nicu, but because it turned out to be the start of a new life for me. The two foreign women who'd arrived in our village started the changes to my life, although it was several years before the really good bit happened. I've got a memory that one of them smelt of

flowers and the other had red hair tied back in a ribbon.
They were both taller than me. (Although most people are
taller than me.) But they were even taller than Adrian.

At first I thought Rita and Angela were the new
leaders of our village. I think that's what the women told me
– people sent by the government to keep order. But they
smiled too much and seemed to like us, so I knew that
couldn't be right. They didn't speak any words I could
understand and I noticed the village people were wary of
them. But back then, everyone was wary of strangers. You
never knew what trouble they could cause. Under Ceausescu
we weren't allowed to have foreigners in our homes or even
speak to them. No wonder we were a bit afraid of Rita and
Angela.

I soon learnt that all the foreign people visiting the
village were called 'volunteers'. That seemed to mean they
gave us things and were kind to us. Lots of them visited that
year. They came from France, Holland, Ireland and
Germany, places I'd never heard of. But one of those
foreigners who'd arrived from England had something in her
eyes that said she would never let Nicu, or anyone else,
harm me. I knew she really liked me and I knew I could trust
her. And that was the moment I knew that I was lucky.

****

I think the most important lesson I absorbed in the early
weeks was never to blame people for anything. It would
have been easy to be judgemental when the true horrors of
the camine revealed themselves but, as we quickly learned,
there is always another point of view. Unexpectedly, I
developed empathy for the women in charge of the

children. They were village women living in abject poverty who were doing their best to earn a pittance to keep their own families afloat. Often they were the sole breadwinner and frequently had an alcoholic husband to contend with. It was easy, in the initial few days, to make snap judgements about anyone who tolerated the conditions in which the children lived. But you needed to balance that view against the indoctrination of a dictator who taught everyone that disability was to be kept hidden from the world. They'd been taught that those children had no value and hence they were kept like animals in cages.

I quickly came to the conclusions that when well-meaning people from wealthy countries start a crusade to 'rescue' human beings from the depths of despair, they need to swallow a huge dose of reality before setting out. We should all take a close look at our motives, try to understand the people we want to help, consider their beliefs and the historical facts and customs of the country. And ask yourself, what is the likelihood of success? Nothing is worse than failure, especially where human lives are concerned. And heaven knows, I faced that prospect often enough.

Deprived children are not cuddly toys or animals, and just for the record, I have never considered taking any of them home. It has always been my firm belief that Romania should be helped to become independent and to look after her own children. To do that, I believe, there needs to be a concerted effort from neighbouring countries to support her. That said, I know children have been adopted abroad and many have been successfully placed.

I mentioned the importance of preparation and, shamefully I can claim very little. A more structured approach to the visit may have given me wings on my heels. But with hindsight, of course, comes a little wisdom.

One of the big questions I often asked myself was – if volunteers succeed in changing the regime, what infrastructure will be in place to support the changes? And for Giurcani, where will those camine children live if someone closes it down? There were probably hundreds of camines all over Romania where children were hidden away like lepers. It was a major goal and not altogether realistic to attempt to bring Romanian lives into line with western civilisation. How could a handful of volunteers change Romanian attitudes to disability? We're not so good at it in our own country, are we? The word hypocrite springs to mind.

In 1991 I made many mistakes. I blush when I remember some of them. I learnt the hard way that foreign aid must both educate and encourage recipients to be pro-active. People living in poverty need to engage with the process of change if it is to be meaningful. They have pride. Even poor people.

Too often I've watched foreigners create mayhem, always with the best of intentions, as they've arrived laden with aid. The material goods have been fought over and stolen and disharmony has washed through village communities as a consequence. I've learnt that giving material possessions is never enough. At the other end of the scale, I met a scary lady who, in the name of 'Christianity', intended to move into the village of Giurcani and 'run it'. That can't be done either. People must run their own lives. Luckily, she soon disappeared. And I'm still trying to get it right after twenty-two years.

****

Dorin

When we shot Ceausescu it was a night I will never forget. But I should go back a week or so before it happened and tell you how it began. I know all about it because I'm a good listener. If the women were gossiping, when they should be working, they often didn't notice if I hung around. I sometimes think that because I've got no hands and feet people think I have no brain either. But I remember things and I'm not afraid to say what I think about life.

I know the trouble started in Timisoara. There was a priest there who spoke out about Ceausescu's bad ways. About him not feeding the people. And then soldiers came to arrest him, because he said what he thought. The people tried to protect the priest but there were a lot of scuffles in the town. The trouble spread and there was another lot of trouble in Iasi, which is only two hours away from Guircani. I heard that the soldiers soon stamped on that and men were sent to prison.

Our night watchman at the camine had a small radio that he used to listen to on his shift. I often sat with him in his hut when I couldn't sleep. I heard the speeches Ceausescu made about how life would soon get better. People told me he built himself a huge palace in Bucharest with more rooms than he could use, while the rest of us were hungry. More than one thousand rooms and some as big as a football field, I was told. What sort of man does that? But we had to be careful what we said because you never knew who was listening. Not that I cared much. What could anybody do to me? I was already stuck in a prison for kids with not enough to eat and a good beating most days.

When the 'big happening' started it was late at night. Violetta, who was married to our watchman Sandu, ran up to the camine with a story that Ceausescu had run away and the people were angry. They were out looking for him, he said. I knew it couldn't be true because no one would dare to chase our leader. Ceausescu was like a god to the people and everyone did what he said, no matter how bad life was. Sandu told Violetta to go back home to their kids and not talk such rubbish, but she told him he would see that she was right in the morning. After she had gone Sandu turned on his radio and we sat and listened in amazement.

After the trouble around the towns, Ceausescu made a broadcast to the people to say there were some 'hooligans' around who were saying bad things about him. No one was to take any notice of them, he said. He promised that he was going to give the people better pensions and good wages and that things were going to get better. But the crowd weren't listening to him. We could hear on the radio that they were booing and jeering him and that they were getting very angry. I couldn't believe how they dared to do that. Everyone listened to him, always. When the crowd became so angry that they were dangerous, the army sent an aeroplane that looked like a big bird into the palace. It swooped down and picked up our

The camine in 1991

Rita visiting the village school in 1991

Angela and Rita enjoy a picnic with the Rotaru family in 1991

Angela and Rita with their hosts the Ursu family in 1991

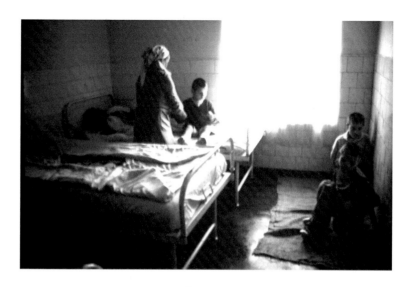

A salon in 1991

1991 – 'my boys' feeding the pigs

Potty success for 'little Adrian'

Fun with balloons with Adrian and the smaller children

Cuddles in the camine kitchen 1992

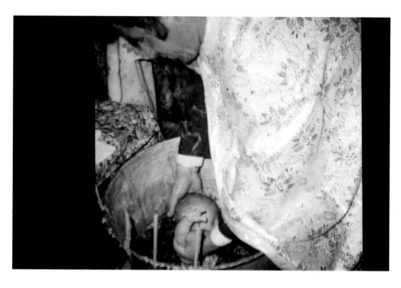

Baby survives the Christening in a bucket!

Daniela seeking our 'lost' Gheorgie

Mariana welcomes the boys to their new home

Rita and the boys having fun in the sun

The boys try Eric's motorbike for size

Dorin meets his birth family

Adrian admiring our hire car

leader and his wife and flew away with them. His three children were not there.

The next day was like no other day in my life. This is what it was like. When the women came to work they were huddled in groups talking about the news. The director told them to get on with their work, but the minute she went back to the office they started talking again. They heard on the news that when the big bird aeroplane dropped Ceausescu and his wife on the ground they were picked up by a small army tank and taken to an army place for safety. People told me you could see it on television. Everyone was so angry that they stormed the place where he was, dragged him and his wife out and on December 25th they shot them. Even that was on TV if you were lucky enough to have one.

Well, no one could believe it. There was singing and dancing in the village for two days. Everyone was drinking and saying that life would now get better. 'Good riddance to Ceausescu!' they shouted. I was glad he was dead. No one felt sorry for him, but no one had any idea what to expect from life in the future either. Who would be put in charge? Who would be our leader?

****

Angela and I were to stay, initially, with Renato's family in the village. His Aunt Johanna worked at the camine as a seamstress although her husband did not appear to have a job.

The home was clean and welcoming. Religious icons of the Russian Orthodox persuasion stared from the walls and evidence of Johanna's artistic talent was everywhere.

Crocheted arm-rests to the chairs, embroidered pictures, rag rugs to the floors; a myriad of colourful items made for interesting inspection.

The house had two kitchens, in-keeping with every other house in the village. One was indoors for cooking in deepest winter and the other, larger one, was outside and used for fine-weather cooking and the preparation and bottling of the summer harvest.

The 'bathroom' was an outdoor plastic water container set above an incongruous bathroom basin. A shelf held the family toothbrushes and there was a mirror for the daughters of the house to check hair and makeup.

Johanna was a quiet slip of a woman with sad, deep brown eyes. She made us welcome in her home and nothing was too much trouble. Sadly, within three years of our arrival her life was claimed by cancer. Shockingly, in that country, there was no medicine available without money to pay for it and that hasn't changed, twenty years later.

Johanna and Costel had two teenage daughters and a son living at home. As with all young people in Romania, they were desperate to learn English and hung on our every word about life in the west. Without a common language we managed to build a relationship with this lovely family. We exchanged English lessons for Romanian vocabulary and I was pleased Angela and I had both brought English/Romanian dictionaries with us.

We slept in clean beds and ate sufficient, if not sophisticated food. I had my water purifying system and Angela and I were determined not to drink the local water unless it was boiled or filtered which proved to be prudent as all water in the village was contaminated. But our caution caused the host family some amusement. They could not work out what we were doing and – well, have you ever tried to explain water purification via a game of charades?

Renato wanted us to meet the camine director while he was around to translate. The director, a lady of some repute around the village, was expecting our arrival. Johanna told us the director had declared to anyone who would listen that she had no idea what foreigners were going to do in her camine or how long they intended to stay. That didn't bode well.

We walked along the village road towards the camine and created a huge amount of interest. Angela suggested royalty couldn't have had a better welcome. Little girls came out of gateways with bunches of wild flowers and a couple of people offered us hospitality of the alcoholic variety which Renato kindly refused, on our behalf. He explained that we were tired but would call to see them another day.

Over the years I've received hospitality and generosity inside those village houses that is humbling. Although Romanian people have little, they are incredibly generous with what they have.

Our meeting with the director was short and cool and neither Angela nor I thought we were going to hit it off with her any time soon. She was polite, but the smile never reached her eyes. She wanted to know why we had come, who was paying us and how old we were. She had a habit of shrugging like a French onion-seller and it was clear she felt that our 'help' was unnecessary. However, her boss, the director in Vaslui, had arranged it and so tolerates us she must. Not a great start. We soon discovered that she was a strong-willed lady and used to getting her own way. (But so was I.) I could envisage tough times ahead if we were to make any changes for the children in her care.

The next day Angela and I said goodbye to Renato and paid him for his invaluable services. As we walked to the camine the following morning we both realised we were now well and truly on our own. It was a warm, late spring day and the rays were welcome on our skin. I remember the sun was warm enough to burn but there was no chance of skin damage where we were going.

We talked a lot about our hopes for the work we intended to do and debated how the staff might treat us. I had paediatric nurse training to fall back on but Angela had a commercial background and was full of concerns about her ability to cope. Would she be strong enough to tackle the task? I privately thought she'd be better than me. I could feel a range of emotions inside me that I thought had been tucked into deep pockets long ago and I was fearful to put my hand in to examine them again. Unwanted children. That was rather too close for comfort. As an illegitimate child who'd known both the fostering, adoption and care system I was suddenly fearful about how I would manage.

We were met in the driveway by a gaggle of the older children, the ones who worked the land we later learned. They spurred us on with gestures and continuous chatter and their excitement about having more foreign visitors was patent. They surely remembered the recent visit from Jane and her friends so expectation of gifts was high. We had a lot to live up to. Luckily I had brought sweets for them and I'd also put crayons and paper in a small rucksack. Angela had packets of balloons and chewing gum. We hoped that would satisfy their expectations.

That first meeting with Adrian, Dorin and Gheorgie was, unknown to me at that time, a monumental moment in my life. They were spotty adolescents with none of the charm of the younger children in the camine who readily won people's hearts with their eyes like melted chocolate. But to me, those teenage boys were the special ones. They were scruffy and shy and probably perplexed as to why anyone would want to be nice to them after a lifetime of neglect. And yes, rather smelly, too.

Looking back, my bonding with them was probably due to my deep love for my own sons who are similar in age. I understand teenage boys. I found I readily identified with all those lost children in a very personal way.

It's strange how challenges and shock can sometimes focus the mind on deep-rooted dilemmas. I remember how, in the quiet moments alone, I tried to realign my entrenched ideas about my accomplishments as a single mother. The boy's father had died when they were young and I'd always thought I should have balanced the need to work and my parenting more successfully. I lacked confidence, particularly as I'd experienced few pointers to good parenting during my own childhood. I often drew comparisons with my son's friends and their families and wished I could have done things differently. But here in

Romania, among the abject conditions for children, I felt like the King Kong of single mothers. I'd definitely got some things right.

Chapter 4

Angela and I decided we would each choose a different salon where eight to ten children were incarcerated. We'd work with our individual children daily in the belief that it would be better to spend most of our time with fewer children if we wanted to make any real headway.

We agreed the children needed to be weaned off the bottles of milk and persuaded to take solid food. But they were so weak and fragile it seemed a monumental task. We also wanted to wash them and try to persuade the women to keep them clean. Clean clothes were needed, which involved a fight with the director who, we discovered, hoarded all donated items like there was no tomorrow. We knew that everything would be an uphill struggle and were beginning to grasp the enormity of the task we had taken on.

****

At the end of the first week the director called us to her office and in a mixture of French and Romanian we worked out that we could no longer stay with our host family in the village. They were, to quote her words, 'not important enough to have foreigners staying with them.' As Johanna was a member of staff at the camine it was tricky to object as we feared there may be reprisals for her if we disobeyed. Could she even lose her job, we wondered.

I suspected there was jealousy afoot. We were paying for our board and lodging and this put the family at an advantage over everyone else in the village. Stupidly, as it turned out, Angela and I allowed ourselves to be ordered to live in the camine where we were given a small side room to share. Maybe they thought it would get rid of us – send us back to England with our tail between our legs. Maybe it was the hope of our rent money being given to the director. Who knows?

The allotted room, which was used as a sewing room by Johanna during the daytime, had two single beds of camine quality and smell and very little else. I remember we dumped our rucksacks on the floor which looked cleaner than the beds and asked ourselves what we had done.

This was to be our new home and how bleak it was. We tried to open the shutters which boarded the filthy single window but were told that we should leave it just as it was. So - small, dark, smelly and soulless was the full extent of what appeared to be our new living space. Gone now was the family welcome and reasonable food; the clean room and the friendship of the lovely Ursu family. Luckily, we both had sleeping bags and we curled inside them to contemplate the future.

That first night of sleeping in the camine was to be my night from hell – the witnessing of the rape of Julian. After that, I knew staying in the camine was not an option.

We were determined to find somewhere else to live and made enquiries around the village. But as strangers in town with a language difficulty, we came up with no results. That wasn't to suggest that by living elsewhere the problems in the camine would go away – far from it. It merely meant we could salvage a degree of sanity each evening in peaceful surroundings while we tried to find a way to move forward and face the many problems.

The next day everyone at the camine was talking about us. Strange, isn't it how you can pick up vibes in any language? It appeared my altercation with the director over little Julian was common knowledge and I learnt that few people ever stood up to her. Now they did. Clearly, raised voices had been heard while I expressed my wrath at the happenings during the night.

Luckily, the deputy director, Lena, came to the rescue regarding our living conditions. She came to find us in the salons that same afternoon and told us she had a neighbour who may be able to help. Lena suggested Angela and I should visit a lady called Maria who might have a spare couple of rooms we could rent.

I think we probably went immediately to find the said Maria. We couldn't bear to wait until the end of the day. I remember Dorin tagged along, assuring us he knew where Maria lived. He never wanted to miss an event and he told us the entire life story of Maria, or so we guessed. He suggested she was *'tock-tock'*, which we took to mean a little on the loony side!

Maria's house was a five minute walk from the camine on one of the back lanes and she met us at the gate which was bolted securely. After some initial garbled discussion, of which we understood nothing, she allowed us in to view the available rooms.

We were offered a room each and a small stove to warm food and boil water. There was a single bed in each room which looked clean; rugs on the floor and an array of religious pictures all over the walls. It seemed Maria was a keen collector of dolls although we were later told they belonged to her daughter who had moved away to get married.

We were delighted with the rooms and agreed to take up Maria's offer that day. I can't remember how we came to agree the rent but it was somehow settled and paid, one week in advance. It was a pittance. Something in the region of ten pounds each for a month.

There were no washing facilities at our new home but we utilised rainwater, collecting it in buckets each time there was a shower. I can remember, shortly after moving in, standing under a leaking gutter during a ferocious storm. I washed my hair and body in exquisite running water. How precious water became that hot summer.

We were given access to the family 'hole in the ground' lavatory. One was much the same as another, we discovered and none had anything to recommend them with the exception of Didi's, which had proper loo roll rather than squares of newspaper.

Maria had a husband called Nicu who was an insignificant man whenever Maria was holding court. But when she was out of the way he was a lovely, gentle man who took delight in having foreign visitors and often gave us produce from his vegetable patch.

I particularly enjoyed Maria's pretty garden which was a blaze of colour, full to bursting with flowers of every variety. Fountains of pink and white, mauves and yellows met the eye from our windows and the evening fragrance from the stocks was especially welcome after a day of hard work in the camine.

We were grateful to be living there. Our landlady was a strange old bird, given to complaining about her hard life. She never grasped that we couldn't understand a word she said. However, as long as we made sympathetic noises in the right places, she was happy.

She often came into our rooms, uninvited, and plonked her large frame on a bed. She always wore a peasant dress of rough, brown cloth, a headscarf of indistinct colour and plastic sandals. She never looked clean, but we soon learnt that standards of hygiene were not high on the priority list of some villagers. Her poor old hands were calloused and grimed with dirt and were, she informed us, full of arthritis. Her ankles were permanently swollen and there was often a distinct odour around her. She died in 2002.

Angela and I devised a washing routine whereby we used rain or well water and doused the flowers with the leftovers. Our clothes were washed in an old enamel bowl with the equivalent of Sunlight soap. The hard bars of waxy soap, which produced very little lather, were the only product we could find when our initial supply was used up. We hung our clothes on the line and marvelled at how quickly everything dried in the hot Romanian sunshine.

Maria and her husband kept chickens and geese which wandered around the garden. Although all gardens in Romanian villages are surrounded by chicken wire and fencing, the little chicks always manage to escape. Maria was forever hunting them down, often not in a very good mood. I'm sure she held us responsible for anything that went missing. She demanded to know many things in a loud and sometimes angry voice and seemed to take our non-communication as a personal affront.

Her attempt to increase the rent was an almost weekly occurrence. Angela was more inclined to stand up to Maria than I and she became something of a bête-noir to our landlady. I witnessed more than one ding-dong battle between them. Nicu and I used to sit and raise eyebrows in amazement at the ability of two women to fight without a common language between them. We never did increase the rent, well, not during that visit, anyhow.

In subsequent years, when I travelled alone, Maria used to blackmail me into giving her more money. I used to justify my soft-heartedness on the basis that life was tough for her, as it was for all villagers and it really wasn't much money to me.

Dorin, Gheorgie and Adrian were regular visitors to our new home. They were fascinated by us and our foreign ways and we had lots of fun with them.

****

Chapter 5

Gheorgie

I don't know much but I know I like the English, 'specially Rita and Eric 'cos they always come back. They come back a lot and always ask what we need. None of the others come back but Rita told me they all have busy lives and lots to do, so I suppose I understand.

I don't remember where I was before I came to Giurcani. I wouldn't like to live in a town because they don't have animals there. I think I like sheep the best. When they're little they're soft and I cuddle them. They smell nice too.

I've been treated badly you know. A lot when I was young. I never thought I'd done anything wrong but I must have or they wouldn't have beaten me. Sometimes they took our food away as punishment. They shouldn't have done that should they? Everyone needs to eat.

****

When I arrived in Giurcani, I didn't know it yet, but my life was about to change. Giurcani was like a caged tiger, waiting to sink her teeth into me. She would quietly reinvent me. And three teenage boys from the camine were shortly to get right under my skin causing an itch that would drive me to lengths I'd never thought possible.

It wasn't that I was unhappy with the life I had, and I certainly wasn't looking for that eureka moment, although I've met a few volunteers who were. This was meant to be an adventure as much as anything, albeit one driven by genuine concern. I felt an urge to do something, for sure,

71

but only intended to do what was possible in the short time I'd allotted myself.

There were many things I didn't know about Romania, probably due to my lack of preparation, and I was in for shocks of Richter scale proportions. I didn't know, for example, that Giurcani sits within one of the poorest regions of Romania. A fault line of communities around Giurcani were shrivelled and desiccated by Ceausescu; worn down by poverty and ill health until all hope was squeezed from their undernourished bodies.

The situation, in varying degrees, was replicated throughout the country. Romanian people were growing old before their time, burdened and bent by too many children and hard physical work. Lack of money and opportunity took its toll. There was no medical care and contaminated water and disease were causing illness and premature mortality.

I visited tumble-down houses with damp, earthen floors and leaking straw roofs where the only furniture was a built-in bed. The fireplaces had long gone cold from lack of firewood. One mug, a plate and fork were often their only possessions. I found it hard to believe that people lived like that in Europe. I had always associated such poverty with third world countries.

I knew little about the politics of the country either, beyond the fact that they shot their dictator on Christmas Day in 1989. But villagers told me, as I started to get to grips with the language, that the new regime was no better than the old. Many of the deposed communist leaders were, reputedly, still in power and for them life was easy.

Everyone knows money and power corrupt in any society on earth. And for the wealthy people of Romania, life was easy. But millions were hungry, particularly in the cities where no crops were grown; jobs were hard to come by and the people were poverty-stricken and frightened.

****

I have a strange fascination for a junk yard of old tractors and machinery not far from Giurcani. For me it's symbolic of a cultural evolution; decades passing under the new democracy. Over the years I've photographed rusty heaps of twisted metal as they've grown ever skywards and one day I asked Didi Rotaru about the increasing size of the dump. He explained that with the fall of communism there was no money to repair anything; no spare parts available for machinery. Manufacturing plants had closed, he told me, jobs lost and the poverty trap was tightening its grip.

Over a decade I saw the flourishing co-operative farms, which once employed thousands in rural areas, diminish at a staggering rate. Where there had been hundreds of acres of food grown on government-owned farms, all tended by machinery, now the land could only be dug by hard, physical labour. Large swathes of corn became a thing of the past. Huge herds of cattle disappeared which affected the meat and milk yield. This in turn impacted on cheese and butter production. Fewer calves were born which prohibited families from buying a cow. Subsistence farming was all that remained on the plots of land the new government had given to rural families. Life was mediaeval.

****

It took a while to get used to the workings of the camine. The women were terrified of the director and sustained verbal lashings from her acid tongue whenever the mood took her. Each day was a struggle for them and for us. Our simplest requests were met with resistance and the women working with the children were bewildered at our attempts to change routines. They were often afraid to comply and insisted everything was channelled through the director. We fully understood their concerns.

We developed a growing relationship with the deputy to the director. She had a daughter training to be a social worker in Vaslui and therefore had some insight into our aims. Her daughter regularly came into contact with distressed children and I think Lena learnt from her that it was time for change. We often wished Lena was in charge of the camine but, to be fair, I don't think the director misunderstood our intentions. She simply preferred the old regime. Making changes took effort and made more work for her and the women.

The camine was teeming with kids and, as the weeks slipped away, we developed relationships with all of them. Gradually we could name them and they began to respond to hugs and kindness.

There were around six of the older ones who worked the farmland and operated the laundry each morning. For them there was freedom from the camine building but it was offset by immensely hard work in all weathers and insufficient food to sustain them. There were many younger ones who ran from room to room in the gloom and for whom life was confined within the building. I never worked out why so many children were kept in those dire conditions when there were acres of outside space. And then there were the bedridden kids, all ages, probably more girls than boys and all with obvious, physical deformities and limitations. No one could tell us the age of any of the children or anything about their backgrounds. The children knew nothing of birthdays, Christmas, their family background or what the future held for them. I guess they all just lived for the day, hoping someone would remember to feed them.

Angela and I slowly came to realise that these children were not 'orphans'. Well, very few. These were society's cast-offs. They were the hidden shame of people indoctrinated by Ceausescu's criminal ethos. They'd all arrived at the gates of Giurcani by one route or another and it would take me many years to piece together the mysteries surrounding them.

Angela and I chose to concentrate our efforts where the children looked most disadvantaged. We felt called by confined scraps of humanity, the embodiment of those media images that Anneka Rice had brought to our attention. Many of those children died over the years and were put to rest in the churchyard next to the camine. Each time I visited I had an update from Dorin on who had died over the past few months. At the very best, one could say that at least they were remembered by others at the camine, if only for a while; and they had a Christian burial. Not much of a legacy for a little life.

We worked hard to build relationships with the women. We hoped that if we worked alongside them we could gradually understand the house rules, start to pick up some Romanian language and gradually change the most offensive regimes. When the women realised that we relieved them of some of their workload they became more responsive.

Over the weeks the staff began to trust us. They smiled a greeting when we arrived each morning and tried to communicate with us. There was laughter at our attempts to speak their language. Some, I believe, even came to like us, although I'm sure they all thought us to be mad. Why would we be there when we were paid no money for our work? What possessed us to live in a foreign country when we belonged in a land of plenty? Charity was an unknown word to them. They were so busy trying to survive that they had never heard of people worse off than themselves. I remember years after those initial visits, I'd taken part in an abseil in Scilly for the Tsunami victims. I took a photo to show the boys which led to all sorts of weird discussions. Why was Rita dangling from a church tower on a piece of rope and how did that help poor people?

Angela and I gradually started to accept invitations into people's homes where we met their families and learnt much about their previous lives under communism. Nothing we heard made easy listening but it was great to finally have more friendships in the village.

Chapter 6

I was keen to release children tied to beds or with hands tied behind their backs but, of course, everything has a consequence. We learned that some were self-harmers, some were violent to small children and some had sexual urges that couldn't be contained any other way. And there was no counselling service or child psychologist on hand to deal with these issues. Life in the camine was a self-perpetuating, vicious circle.

And then there was the feeding regime. We had so little time to make a difference in our chosen salons that there was no time for a softly, softly approach. But it was essential to try to keep on good terms with the director. Our differences needed to be put aside. At times, we wondered if it was a 'woman thing'. It was particularly obvious that she dealt with men in a very charming way. I could almost like her at those moments. But maybe, if I'd been in her shoes, I'd have been resentful, too. We were thrust upon her and her world was opened up to foreign scrutiny. It couldn't have been a good experience, particularly as loss of face is a huge issue in Romania. We challenged her practices while her staff looked on.

Little by little we started to pick up Romanian words and phrases. The older kids soon grasped the game of naming objects for us and our pronunciation caused hilarity. We reciprocated by naming objects in English and teaching them nursery rhymes and children's songs. They were surprisingly quick to learn and were also learning to have fun, probably for the first time in their lives.

We met, briefly, two French women who visited the camine. Their remit was to oversee initial explorations for bringing water into the building from a bore hole on a distant hill. They worked for a French charity called Equilibre and it was their intention to return to the camine when drilling started. Results of the investigations showed there was sufficient water available and they planned to build bathrooms, for which rooms were set aside. We were thrilled. This would be a huge benefit to our efforts to keep the children clean.

A massive amount of work was undertaken by the French and at great expense. Indoor plumbing appeared over the next year; sparkling white wash-basins and showers to a standard I would welcome in my own home. The sad outcome was that no water ran through the pipes after about one month and the brand new bathrooms were never used again.

****

I chose a room and set to work. It was a typical cramped salon with rusty cots, little light and no fresh air. I was horrified to discover from one of the women that these children were, in fact, seven or eight years old. I remember my disbelief and a lot of finger counting went on to establish the facts. Of course, when I thought about it further, I realised that they all had full sets of second teeth, bearing out the information. In a way, they were quite scary; minute, frail and with large teeth in big heads.

I started work by drawing a picture of a bottle of milk to be placed above each cot. I marked a large X through the bottle to imply no milk should be given to this child. I discovered the Romanian word for bottle was 'sticla'. In felt pen I wrote *'no sticla'* on the notice.

I ventured into the kitchen and met a lovely lady called Natalie who was the camine cook. Her smile was open and after some communication by hand gestures, I was delighted to find an old-fashioned, metal, mouli-mincer among her utensils. I asked if I could sieve some of the vegetable soup she was keeping warm in a massive saucepan. As she continued to smile I took advantage of her good nature and proceeded to sieve some of her soup into dented metal bowls for the children in my room. The sieving created a thickened mixture which would stand me in good stead for what was to come. And what a pantomime that turned out to be.

I propped the weak little things up on pillows, wedging them into the corner of the cots. As they were unable to support their own body-weight they frequently toppled over which caused them, and me, distress. I asked Angela if she would help me and together we started the process of feeding the children with their first taste of solid food.

It was surreal. I was spat and screamed at by very obstinate children who objected to baby food being pushed into their mouths. Where their strength came from I'll never know. The clash of spoon on teeth was nerve-jingling. Angela held their arms under a sheet to aid the process and, with perseverance over a number of days, they gradually took the food.

We found bowls and buckets in which we collected water to wash the children. We enticed the director to give us clothes from her store in an attempt to keep them clean and dry. And we introduced them to play, using balloons and singing songs to which we clapped with huge enthusiasm.

Much to the astonishment of the staff, Angela and I worked from eight o'clock in the morning, which was breakfast time, until after the children had supper. We were determined to supervise their meals. Even on Sundays we visited the children – there was absolutely nothing else to do in the village – and little by little the feeding regime of our two salons improved. If I had known that it was the start of a new life for some of those little ones, I would have been more encouraged. However, I had no idea on that first visit that over the years these children would strengthen from their new diet and some would eventually learn to walk.

The days passed, one very much like another. When I look back I realise it was a hard, daily grind. Washing, feeding, potty-training and stimulating the children was a full-time job and the environment we worked in was stinking and generally unpleasant. But the highlight of our day could be something as simple as a smile from a child who had previously never given us eye contact. Maybe a child would reach out needy arms to us, anxious to be picked up. Cause for celebration indeed. Those things would lift our spirits. We'd share the news with each other and talk about it for hours.

Chapter 7

In 1991, the border with Russia was a mere three miles from Giurcani, although the bordering country is now known as Moldova. I remember the sense of curiosity and slight fear that Russia's proximity prompted. (I'd probably read too many Cold War spy stories.) I wanted to take a look, to glimpse the harsh, tail-end of Europe. However, I was assured by villagers that although I could cross the border into Russia with ease, I would not be allowed back into Romania.

The military presence on the border confirmed the advice and the weapon-wielding soldiers suggested it would not be prudent to try. It certainly put another slant on life and my curiosity waned overnight. Lost in Russia was one step too far, even for me. I did, from time to time, see small groups of men, said to have slipped over the border into Romania at night. They carried an array of trashy trinkets to sell to destitute villagers. I was assured that life in parts of Russia was worse than the poverty in Romania. This was hard to grasp, living as I was among such hardship and deprivation. There was an incongruity about people wanting to escape *to* Romania when we all wanted to alleviate Romania's suffering. 'Had we got it wrong?' I asked myself more than once.

****

I received hospitality around the village in the early years, not all of it pleasurable, it has to be said. I was living amongst austerity and, shockingly, few families in the village knew anything but extreme poverty. They lived literally from hand to mouth and the entire food source for their families was produced on their land. There was a bartering system running throughout the village which brought small variations to the diet.

The hard work of cultivation and planting of crops fell mainly to the women and, of course, everything was entirely weather-dependent. There was no access to pesticides and the fertilisers were basic, animal dung. The land was never replenished with minerals or phosphates and the regular lack of rain could ruin entire crops.

Animals were reared in back yards: pigs, sheep, chickens, ducks, geese and there also, lived the essential guard dogs of all shapes and colours. Chickens were killed by the women on an ad hoc basis and went into tasty stews and soups. The killing of the pig or sheep, by the man of the house, was a huge family occasion and only took place once or twice a year. The animal was slaughtered by slitting its throat and it was then hung from the nearest tree. Here it would drip blood for many hours before the knife went in to butcher it into sizable chunks. The offal was fried, flesh was roasted or minced and the intestines used to make delicious sausages. There was always a feast for the family on the day of the slaughter, but much of the meat was either salted or frozen to provide for the coming months.

Fruit and vegetables were grown throughout the spring and summer and the women preserved them in brine or syrup in large, air-tight, glass jars. Tomatoes, aubergines, courgettes and corn were stored until winter in underground cellars which were cool all the year round. I remember one hot summer I arrived as the water melon season was at its best. Huge chunks of reddish-pink flesh were served up by Tori and we devoured them in the garden while listening to the hum of Didi's bees. The village women made their own tomato puree too and they pickled eggs, gherkins and onions.

There was no shop in the village in the early years and a trip to Birlad was difficult and costly. Even those who travelled to Birlad found nothing but jars of vegetables and tins of miserable, pallid meat to purchase. The shops were unwelcoming, dark and barely worth the visit. Bread was queued for in towns and butter was non-existent. Chickens were bred in country homes for both eggs and meat but I have never eaten such tough chicken in all my life. Talk about old boilers!

The women were bread, cake and cheese makers. They produced a grey, solid version of bread which was served daily without butter or margarine. I never learned to love it. I believe I dreamed about fresh bread with lashings of butter. The cheese was a non-matured type called *brunsa* which was a basic curd strained through muslin and eaten immediately. In later years, when we managed to get the boys making cheese, much interest was shown in English cheese cultures that were matured for flavour.

Another delicacy offered for special occasions was pig's trotter in aspic jelly. On one occasion Angela and I were invited to eat with a village family. Upon arrival it was obvious we were the only people to eat at the table. The meal was set in the front room and we were seated like royalty, to be waited upon by the women and children.

As if that wasn't embarrassing enough, I shall never forget the arrival of the pig's trotter. It was a huge honour, so I later learned from Didi, to be offered such revered food. But I thought I would be sick. I was horrified. This lump of pale-skinned, hoofed flesh was sitting in yellow gunge and daring us to reject it. The kindness of the family and our inbuilt manners didn't allow us to offend them. Luckily, by this time there was a little trick we'd learned. I always kept a surgical glove in my pocket in which I could secrete unwanted food, thus avoiding hurt to the wonderful, generous host families. A trotter in aspic jelly was one step too far for both of us. I declared I would turn vegetarian for the remainder of the visit. I'm ashamed to say that two of that particular pig's trotters went uneaten. The meat, however, slipped from the bone with ease and then into a surgical glove.

Much was made of drinking home-made *suica*, especially by the men folk who distilled it in their back yards. It's a plum-based liqueur, very potent and in my view, disgusting to taste. In the early years much pressure was put on me to partake and Romanians have a way of feigning disapproval over refusal about such matters. However, as the years went by I noticed Tori always refused alcohol and was never chastised. When I asked how she avoided it she told me that ladies of a 'certain age' were excused the vagaries of potent drink. Needless to say, I never drank it again.

The great joy about taking hundreds of photos over the years is they jog your memory about so many things, including lots of happy occasions when the generous people of Giurcani allowed me the privilege of joining their family celebrations.

During one of my early visits to Giurcani, when my understanding of the language was still limited, I was invited to attend a christening in the nearby village of Pecan. A time and place was set for meeting the family and I was duly waiting, as instructed. An ancient, rusty tractor chuffed up the road and aboard was the grandmother of the baby with a large bunch of flowers in her hand. Alongside her were the mother and her baby who was resplendent in ribbons and a white, knitted shawl. They drew up alongside me and hailed me aboard. I was a little taken aback by the mode of transport but entered into the spirit of the occasion and travelled slowly to Pecan for the service.

Upon arrival at the church we were greeted by other members of the family and friends who had travelled ahead of us by horse and cart. Together we entered the church and stood around in readiness for the ceremony. The priest, a young man I had met many times, was very rosy cheeked and it soon became apparent that he was the worse for drink. The baby, no more than a couple of months old, was prepared for the water blessing by being undressed down to her nappy. A huge, metal bucket of cold water was placed on the floor and the priest proceeded to dunk the baby right under the water, three times. I was petrified he would drop her or even drown the small scrap such was his liquor-fired enthusiasm. But, apart from some loud wailing the child appeared to be none the worse for the experience.

Another occasion that springs to mind was a wedding Angela and I were invited to. We had nothing to give to the happy couple apart from American dollars so we shared out the agreed amount and set out to join the celebrations. How embarrassing for us! We mistook the bridesmaid to be the bride and donated our generous gift to the wrong person. However, unable to right the mistake we danced the night away and ate copious amounts of food. Neither Angela nor I have a very developed sense of rhythm and we caused much laughter as we attacked the local two-step with gusto. There was singing and more drinking until the dawn came up. We had a wonderful time.

****

One day, when Angela and I had been in the village for about four weeks we had a lovely surprise. Adrian ran into the camine with a look of excitement. 'Come quick! Come quick!' he gabbled and dragged me by the hand, out into the boiling hot sunshine. Dorin was not far behind and I believe Ionelle and Gheorgie brought up the rear.

Angela and I watched in amazement as a massive four-by-four, left-hand drive vehicle swept up the drive in a flurry of dust and came to a halt right in front of us. We waited for a man and woman to get out. They were clearly not Romanian; a middle-aged couple with beaming smiles stood in the oppressive sun and extended their hands in greeting.

'Are you English?' the man asked with a foreign accent. I agreed we were and waited for him to introduce himself. It transpired that Dr. Jan Broeders, together with his wife Yvonne were working for the Dutch Red Cross on an Aid Programme. Jan is a special needs expert and has offered his knowledge to the Dutch Red Cross on many occasions. He has worked in South America as well as Europe. Over the years we would become good friends and the longer I know Jan the more respect I have for his charity work.

Jan had heard a chance remark in a camine near Vaslui that two English women were working in Giurcani. He was curious about which organisation was supporting us so he and his wife had come to find out. He was shocked to discover that we were two lone voices, working in a wilderness.

Angela and I had seen no one except the Romanian villagers for weeks and we were excited to have visitors who spoke English. But better was to come. Jan suggested that as we had no official organisation to support us we should spend the coming weekend in Iasi with his team of eleven Dutch volunteers. He offered us rooms at the hotel where he and his volunteers lived and promised us a fun weekend away. How good that sounded! We had experienced a huge amount in those first few weeks in the camine, but fun was not part of it.

It was with interest we watched him charm the director. She smiled and entertained him to coffee and biscuits and made an invitation for him to visit at any time. She personally showed him and Yvonne around the camine. In later years Jan welcomed the camine director to Holland to see the work he did with special needs children. Sadly no changes appeared in Giurcani as a result.

True to his word, Jan arrived the following Friday to collect us and we left the village for the first time in over a month. We were like a couple of kids. Jan told us that he had been working in Romania for many months and had set up support projects in five camines. His volunteers were all special needs teachers working with the children each day while living in a hotel in Iasi. How lucky they were.

When we arrived at the Hotel Moldova we were amazed by its facilities. We each had an en-suite bedroom with hot and cold running water and a clean double bed. We were introduced to the Dutch volunteers who spoke excellent English and we spent many hours chatting about shared experiences, theirs being very similar to ours. We really liked them.

We were offered a tour of the city and it started next door to the hotel. We'd noticed the impressive, turreted building which was, we learned, the Palace of Culture. Inside, it had room after room of art and museum pieces, all set around a grand staircase. It seemed odd to us that only one or sometimes two light bulbs graced impressive chandeliers. One bulb was lit where there could have been ten which made the place gloomy and far from ideal for viewing the treasures. Jan explained that electricity was expensive and even public buildings had to make savings.

We loved Iasi. It was the first time I'd had to deal with a tram system and I found it a bit scary having to consider tramlines as well as traffic when crossing roads. The city has a dazzling array of churches, each with the ornate interior I came to expect from an Orthodox church.

Tree-lined streets; a zoo and park, poor, downtrodden people and Dacia cars - Iasi had it all. Even pollution. I was surprised to find so much smog after the fresh air of Giurcani.

The fact that we had hot running water and a shower was a treat, but when we realised we would be living on Dutch food, brought overland by Jan for his volunteers, we were in heaven. They produced jars of thick chocolate spread and cream biscuits and cheeses. It was wonderful. We spent time between each others' rooms, exchanging backgrounds and sharing jokes. We were surprised to find that all the volunteers were receiving their full salaries from their jobs in Holland while they volunteered in Romania. What a far cry from our own situation.

We went out to dinner on the Saturday night. Jan and Yvonne chose a smart restaurant in another part of town which was attached to a hotel. I don't remember exactly what we ate but I do remember the attentive service from staff and the friendship of lovely Dutch people, which we appreciated so much. We were like dried-out sponges, soaking up superb hospitality and the fun of being in touch with English-speaking people, if only for a short while.

On the Monday morning Jan offered to show us some of their projects. We visited three camines that were being supported by the Dutch Red Cross and were staggered by what we found. Under their care, each one had evolved into childcare facilities near to European standards. The Dutch volunteers were doing an excellent job with the children, offering physiotherapy, food programmes and medical care.

We had a great time with the Dutch Red Cross and saw them many times after our first meeting.

Chapter 8

Eventually it was time to return to England and take up my post as a Dame at Eton College. I think, on reflection, that our three months in the camine were worthwhile. But when I left those children I already knew that I would return. Something about the older boys, in particular, was already under my skin. The injustice of their lives kept me awake at night. Angela felt the same and at some point we hatched a plot to return for Christmas.

I left the camine with certain changes in place. Many of 'my' children were being fed a regular diet of baby food and some were showing signs of improved health. A few had learned to sit up and two had made efforts to crawl. Angela had similar successes. But I was worried that all the progress would be lost if the bottles of milk were re-instated, although I was tentatively confident that some of the women might continue our work. They had come to understand our motives and were helpful in sieving the food and even feeding the children. Now was the time for a little faith.

Leaving was heart-breaking. I watched those older boys wave goodbye and sobbed. Had we done harm? Had we shown them something we couldn't sustain? Had we raised expectations only to dash them? I couldn't answer those questions any more than I knew what the future held.

Back in the real world I knew I was going to have difficulty slipping into what used to be the normality of my life. Over the three months at the camine my Romanian had improved, allowing me to even start thinking in Romanian.

When I arrived home I found that I sometimes had to pause to find the right English word. Ridiculous! However, I had no trouble adjusting to a more interesting diet and never once hankered after village food.

Friends on the islands had arranged a welcome home BBQ for me at the home of the lovely John Hicks. Sadly I was fog bound in Penzance and unable to enjoy it. But, as islanders always say, 'That's island life.'

But the wealth and opulence of Eton was another matter altogether. I had grasped the basics of college life at my interview and knew I was about to enter a privileged lifestyle that few have the fortune to experience. But, as yet, I had no idea just how remarkable that lifestyle would be.

****

Over the next few years I travelled regularly in and out of Romania, utilising my generous school holidays. And there was always a fundraising project afoot. Friends, old and new, were supportive.

Every time I visited the children of Giurcani a new need was identified. A playroom was created by Dutch volunteers. Educational toys, walking aids, wheelchairs and money for food and medicines were provided by the English. New flooring, clothes, washing powder – the list was endless. The new extension was completed by Marks and Spencer but sadly another twenty children arrived to fill the space. Not what they had hoped for.

But after a few years, when the other volunteers had ceased to return to the village, I became something of a lonely, one-woman crusade. I was now staying with Didi and Tori Rotaru rather than returning to the home of Maria. It was a friendlier environment and the food was good!

I had become deeply attached to three teenage boys, Adrian, Dorin and Gheorgie who worked harder than any men I'd known. They spent hour upon hour hoeing the land and planting crops. They fed the animals, fetched and carried for anyone, washed the camine floors and laundered the clothes which they hung on wire fences to dry. And poor Adrian had to work in the director's home too. The reward for all their labour was minimal amounts of food and no thanks for anything they did. But it was noticeable that no one ever beat them when I was around; one small victory. I believed that those boys, more than any others in the camine, could have managed to live outside of institutional life, if only a small wind of opportunity passed their way.

Over the years I had deeply rewarding times with those lads. They heaped spade-loads of joy on me each time I visited. I loved the days when I took the small children out into the sunshine and the boys joined me, sneaking away from their duties and keeping an eye open for the wrath of the director. They enjoyed the crayons and colouring books I brought for the younger children, taking great care to colour between the lines. I could hardly watch Dorin. His concentration and dexterity with just two digits brought tears to my eyes. That lad never allows his disabilities to impede his progress in anything.

I took balsa wood airplanes, footballs, bubbles, tee shirts and caps, footwear and jumpers – all manner of things to perk up the children's' lives a little. It was heart-breaking to realise they'd missed their childhood and their adult lives held no promise whatsoever. No one wanted them; no one cared if they lived or died. Well, now I cared and dozens of friends were at home to support me.

Often the three boys talked about wanting a life outside the camine and exuded a longing you could taste. They told me they saw kids in the village return to their families after school and noticed families at weddings, all taking care of each other. No one beat village kids, they said, and they didn't want to be beaten any more either. But I knew they had no hope of being fostered or adopted. No one wanted uneducated, teenage boys with spots and health problems.

Camine children were stigmatised just as illegitimate children had suffered in the post-war years in Britain. I was one of those children and I knew how it felt to be shunned for things that weren't my fault. But I believe I nurtured a germ of an idea to help those boys. Not a fully formed idea but something that niggled at my brain, itching to get out. Something was bubbling away on the back burner and before I knew it, my head and my heart would sign up to a life-time commitment. Like Topsy, my love for those lads just grew.

****

I travelled in and out of Romania, sometimes three times a year. I sampled all the seasons and celebrated Easter, All Saints Day, very important in the Russian Orthodox calendar, and two Christmases in the village. Every time I took as many gifts as I could carry and always money to meet the necessities for the children.

The welcome at Didi and Tori's home was always warm and the friendship grew each year. I noticed the boys had started to visit them, too. They did small jobs around the house and garden in return for a generous plate of food and kind words.

Every time I visited, the boys reiterated their desire to move out of the camine. The only realistic option ahead of them, from the government's point of view, was transfer to an adult institution and I knew that would be the end of their dreams. I'd visited a couple of those places with the Dutch Red Cross and could never allow the boys to be incarcerated in such establishments.

But as each year passed I knew the boys' fate was moving ever nearer. They were already too old to be in a camine for children and each time I left, I wept for them, always fearful they would be spirited away before my next visit.

As the years slipped by it became obvious to me that much of the work I did in the camine was being wasted. My efforts were spread too thinly. The task was too vast for me to make an impression on my own. I discussed my concerns with Jan Broeders and Didi and both agreed I was right. The initial influx of help had long gone and it was obvious the old regimes were slipping back – they were easier for staff to manage. Much of my teaching of new methods was becoming a thing of the past. Except, I noticed, the children that Angela and I had spent so much time with. They were definitely holding their own.

I noticed the content of the playroom gradually disappeared. Little by little the toys and books went missing; soft toys and wall decorations were nowhere to be found. 'They wore out,' I was told. On one visit, the washing machine and tumble drier that I'd raised funds for a couple of years earlier had broken. I was willing to have them repaired but soon they too disappeared. The television I'd bought for the older boys' salon disappeared along with a CD player bought to amuse the bed-ridden children. Another time the horse had died and they were struggling to collect clean water from the well. The children were drinking contaminated water and the neglect was tangible.

There was, however, one bright spot for me. One year when I arrived, unannounced, I was met with a sight in the village that reduced me, yet again, to tears. For there, outside the school railings and walking in crocodile formation were six of the children from my salon. I also recognised a few of Angela's children, too. They were supervised by one of the women from the camine who smiled with delight and engulfed me in a bear-hug embrace.

Those puny children Angela and I had taken off bottles of milk were right before me. Not only were they walking, but they had smiles and hugs for me that melted me quicker than the summer heat. What a joy. I had continued to work with the same children over the years and knew some were close to walking, but what a wonderful sight that was. I floated on air for a couple of days. I told myself to count the blessings and not to dwell on what I saw as failures. A French lady once told me, 'In Romania we do as we can. We are like a dripping tap.' I took that to mean little steps should be celebrated. And celebrate I did. I praised the staff for their excellent work and thanked them for staying true to my aims in my absence.

It was always a joy to be welcomed back. Catching up with the older boys always took time as they wanted to relay every single happening since my last visit. A woman had been sacked; a foreign visitor had been; a child had died or a village wedding had been celebrated. All these things impacted on their lives.

****

Gheorgie

Rita used to tease me and sing songs. I still know the English words to 'Row, row, row the boat'. Umm... I remember we also played with balloons. I'd never seen a balloon and when my one went bang she really laughed. She wasn't even cross. She blew some air into another one for me. And there were magic bubbles. You just blew at a stick and they floated in the air. I never worked out how that happened. We used to play clapping games and I always managed to clap at the wrong time. Sometimes Rita laughed until she cried. I didn't understand that either.

We used to have crayoning books and I loved learning to draw between the lines. Angela helped as well. We'd stick the pictures on the camine walls. The women used to say things like, 'You're behaving like a kid. Five-year-olds do colouring, not stupid great lumps like you.' I must have been about sixteen or seventeen at the time. But I didn't care. I loved my pictures and they gave me a good feeling inside. No one could take that away from me.

I used to take Rita to see the baby pigs sometimes. And the calves. Umm...I remember one day it was time to kill a pig and the men came and cut the pig's throat in front of her. She was a bit upset but it's the way we do things in Romania. It's always a good day when we kill a pig. Rita said she couldn't bear the smell of the blood that ran through the dust near her feet. Everybody (well, not us kids at the camine – not very often anyway) gets a small piece of meat when a pig is killed. It's a real treat. The men burn all the hair off the pig with matches and then strip the skin with sharp knives. They eat it straight from the pig. I thought Rita would be sick that day, years ago. I often wonder what they eat in England. They have lots of funny ways, the English.

One year I remember Rita came for Christmas. And Angela. We had never heard of Christmas. We made decorations from pretty paper and we put them up in the play room. There was a present for every kid in the camine that year. And we had a shiny tree with decorations on it.

Chapter 9

Upon meeting 'my Romania boys' you can be entranced by dancing blue eyes or a cavernous grin. You may be taken with a sharp mind and sharp tongue which demands to know all about you. But one of the last things you notice is their special needs.

Adrian is the eldest. We discovered he was already twenty when we first met him in 1991. I thought he was about thirteen. He's a shrimp of a fellow with a shock of muddy-blond hair and blue eyes, bright and clear as a robin's egg. He's quiet and thoughtful and shy in his manner of speech, often lowering his eyes under his thatch of spiky hair. In Romania his colouring is usually attributed to Hungarian blood lines, but who knows where Adrian's heritage lies?

In the early years I developed an affinity with his quiet ways and charm. He was always willing to run errands and nothing was ever too much trouble. One day I discovered he had a beautiful tenor voice. With a little encouragement he sang Romanian folksongs for me which he'd learned at village celebrations where he'd lingered in the shadows, tolerated if he behaved well. He was eager to learn English songs, too, which he learnt by rote from my own, dubious renditions.

In more recent years, his desire to sing has passed and he has put away other childish delights such as colouring books and puzzles. To be truthful, these days, he resembles a little, wizened old man. A hard life and decades of malnutrition and deprivation have taken their toll on

Adrian, more so than the other two. I fear he may not live to be a great age. He suffers from frequent headaches and poor teeth; numerous dental extractions and painful treatment have resulted in a fear of the very mention of the dentist. He now has little left in his poor gums to get to grips with the meat he so enjoys, but still he smiles that gappy smile that tears at my heartstrings.

Dorin comes next in age. He was nineteen when I arrived but looked much younger. He has physical disabilities but a scalpel-sharp brain. He deserved the opportunity to go to school but when Didi offered him reading classes as an adult, he had no heart to study. He's constantly enquiring, as bright as a button and will never accept half a truth or half a story.

There is a standing joke before we make a visit to the village: how long will Dorin's list of wants be this year? Not only does he have 'needs' but he offers reasoned arguments about why we should provide his chosen delights. But, to be fair, he is always prepared to wait, often for many years, while money is raised to pay for things.

Gheorgie is the youngest and the least able of the three. He has a lovable face despite his rather large ears and wonky teeth and he smiles from morning till night. He doesn't like to be rushed and too much hustle and bustle gets him agitated. He loves feeding the chickens and geese, collecting the eggs and shutting the fowl in the coop at night to avoid the marauding fox. He takes great delight in the birth of new animals and spends a lot of time grooming the horse. He can get cross with Adrian for drinking alcohol and raises his finger to admonish him, rather like an angry parent.

****

Dorin

I don't have any memories before life in the village of Giurcani, although I've learnt in recent years that I lived with my mother in Vaslui until I was two. Until Rita and Eric came to Giurcani and rescued us from the camine, we never even knew how old we were. When they got our paperwork from the authorities they discovered our birthdays, and every year we get birthday cards from them and have a drink to celebrate.

I want to tell you about the place I knew as home for the first twenty-six years of my life and why I was still in a camine for kids when I was in my twenties. I was a good worker, you see, and my labour came free of charge. For that reason alone I had a value and therefore I wasn't sent to an Adult Institution.

The camine held something in the region of seventy-five kids of all ages. We were all classed as having learning disabilities. (I think that's what the volunteers called it, anyway.) But all we knew, back then, was that 'we weren't quite right in the head' and 'couldn't live out in the community.' The staff told us we were 'mad'. Strange as it may sound, that wasn't of much consequence to us. We just accepted life as it was. .

The most important things in our lives, back then, were the need for food (we were always hungry), managing to avoid another beating (they came thick and fast), and the constant worry of how much work was in store for us on any day of the week. And of course the bloody cold Romanian winters. We have mountains of snow every year. Winter was always a worry, especially for me 'cos I had no winter boots to fit my stumps and they used to get red raw with weeping chilblains. When you haven't got proper hands or feet you are likely to get bashed about a bit. Sometimes my stumps were so cut and sore I had to stay in bed.

All the days were the same back then. Work, hunger, beatings and the occasional laugh when we managed to get one over on the staff, or maybe grab a miserable bit of meat when it was thrown into the soup. The days just came and went. The camine was a shit place, I suppose. Everyone worked hard, except the kids who were tied to their beds.

A boy called Constantine, who was about sixteen when Rita arrived, used to smash the glass in his salon window and then cut himself with the broken bits. I remember he did it one day when a volunteer was playing with a kid in the same room. He just sliced his arm, really deep, and then started to cut his legs to shreds. The volunteer screamed and called Rita 'cos she used to be a nurse. She came in with a box with a cross on the lid. The thing I really thought was strange was her putting on rubber gloves before she tried to clean up Constantine's wounds. I've never worked that one out to this day.

Rita told the director that he needed to go to hospital. But when she took a look she just shrugged and said there was no need for that. Anyway, there was no transport to take him to Birlad so he had to manage the best he could. Rita had some strips which she managed to get on to some of the cuts. We had to help her by holding

Constantine down as he fought everyone he came in contact with. And he used to bite like a dog. Dan sat on him and he's big. After the strips were put on, Rita bandaged his wound and then the director said he had to have his hands tied behind his back for four days so that he didn't pull the bandages off. Rita was really shocked.

Night time in the camine was tough 'cos you couldn't sleep for more than half an hour at a time. It used to get dark and quite spooky 'cos we had no outside lights and all the inside lights would be switched off or there was no electric. But there was always loads of noise and lots of shadows.

There was always screaming from the small kids' salons, I suppose because of their growling hunger or from lying in the stinking piles of shit in their cots. They'd cry and nobody ever came. Eventually they'd stop screaming and sleep a bit. The older kids, those not locked in rooms for their own safety, rampaged around beating small children, lashing them to the beds and buggering the unlucky. It was the same thing that happened to me, Adrian and Gheorgie when we were little and we just had to accept it.

One day Rita caught us buggering and beating kids. She was so angry I've never forgotten it. That was the first time anyone told us it was wrong. Now I'm grown- up I can see the harm in it, but back then it was just done for amusement. Stuff like that used to interrupt your sleep 'cos you had to look out for your own safety. As I grew older I was one of the power groups meting out the punishment, being top dog, but in my younger days life wasn't easy for me with no hands and stumpy feet. But it made me strong and some say it made me gobby. I'm never lost for words – not me.

I've been told that I could easily have learned to read and write if I'd had hands and feet. That's what made them stick me in a camine. My only problem seems to be a lack of schooling and opportunity. There's nothing wrong with my brain! Nobody had opportunities in our village back then, so I'm not alone there.

I'm told I was a cute little kid and during my first year or so in the camine the director used to keep me in her office while she worked. I remember she shared her biscuits with me. I used to crawl around the floor and play with pens and things but I guess, eventually, I grew too troublesome. By the time I was four years old she released me to fight my corner among the bullies in the main wing.

Kids were divided into sleeping salons according to what they could do. The volunteers said the rooms were stinking. I've even seen them breathe into a hanky, it was so bad. I can't say I ever noticed. It was just the smell I grew up with.

It didn't take long for me to see what my fate would be if I didn't learn to walk on my stumpy feet. Up to that point, a shuffle on my backside was as good as it got, gathering the filth and dust from the floors as I went. It used to make my arms hurt and even bleed as I used them to navigate my way around. But I was determined to get upright, no matter how hard it was or how long it took. Learning to walk was also important so I could grab my share of the food. I saw what happened to kids who had their food stolen. They got really skinny and couldn't walk.

They had to stay in cots all day and all night with a bottle of milk thrown at them every now and then. I wasn't going to be one of them. I'd seen loads of them die and get buried in the churchyard at the back of the camine. I taught myself to use the lavatory, too. I didn't want to be one of the stinking kids who sat in their own filth all day. Wiping my ass isn't easy with no hands - I'll leave you to imagine how I do that!

I learned to stand by hanging on to the babies' cots. I used to slide along sideways, despite the pain from the bleeding chunks of flesh that I call feet. Sometimes, when I was lucky, I'd be given a pair of trainers that were huge, but I was able to stuff my feet into.

The worst thing, even worse than deep snow, was tramping through the shit that surrounded the outdoor lavatories, holes in the ground used by kids and staff. Even volunteers had to use them and as there weren't any doors, just three brick walls around a hole, it caused us kids much amusement. We used to burst into applause when they achieved their goals. It amused me that even visitors had to use the same lavatories we did.

Of course, I never learnt to wash my fingers or stumps, water was too precious for that, and stomach problems were rife amongst the inmates, vomit adding to the stench in the camine. My bleeding feet got infected more times than I can remember. Most times I didn't get to see a doctor and the scabs kept weeping and falling off – or I picked them.

I grew up used to nasty comments, threats and beatings. They were part of everyday life for us older boys, those who actually got outside the living block each day to work in the fields on the small farm. I grew up to be strong, partly because I learnt to steal food from other kids. I reckoned I was entitled to it as they stayed indoors all day doing nothing and I had to go outside and work. If I could learn to walk, I thought, so could they. Not that I would have changed places with them.

Mostly the women turned a blind eye to my antics, but from time to time I'd catch them on a bad day and they'd beat me hard. I always laughed no matter how much they hurt me 'cos I saw how mad it made them.

The camine director was a strong woman. She ruled with a rod of iron and the women and us kids were afraid of her. But I knew how to get the staff in trouble if they were shitty to me. I'd tell tales to the director and then stand back and watch the results. She would really shout at them and I've lost track of the number I've seen her sack. There were always loads more women in the village who wanted to earn regular money 'cos there was no other work. The women learnt to respect me, in a small way.

The director spread all sorts of information around the place, true or false – no one ever knew. Instructions had arrived, she'd tell us, from the powers on high. 'If we don't scrub all the rooms with disinfectant in the next week we would have evening food stopped until further notice.' Another one was, 'Anyone caught nicking food will be sent to Husi.' Husi was the dread of all the older kids. It's an institution for adults with a fearsome reputation. We still managed to nick a few chunks of bread when her back was turned. She often used to sneak home early and take Adrian with her. He had to do her housework and feed her animals.

106

She never paid him, but sometimes gave him some wine. Rita thinks that's why he has a drink problem now he's older, but I wouldn't like to say.

Once she told us the volunteers were 'communist spies' and we, like puppets on a string, believed her for a day or two. It was only in later years that I realised she spoke no English and couldn't translate anything they said. Despite her best efforts, it didn't take long for the foreigners to win us over with the stuff they brought and we loved the attention they gave us.

****

Adrian

I knew that I shouldn't still be at Guircani when I was already twenty-something but no one told me to go anywhere else, so I stayed. I'm a good worker. Even the director said that and I think that's why she kept me at the camine. I used to go to her house and dig her garden and sweep her paths. She used to give me a bottle of beer or some wine if I worked hard all day.

I was in charge of the camine cow which was kept for milk. Every morning I had to take the cow down to the village where a man collected it and took it to graze on the hills with other peoples' animals. When they came back in the evening I had to milk it and take the bucket of milk to the kitchen.

Sometime we had pigs, too. I loved the baby ones and I used to take a long time when I was sent to feed them. Sometimes I would get in the pen with them. They smelt nice and were always warm. Even in winter.

I can't remember a time when I wasn't at the camine. Like most kids I was there 'cos I'm handicapped. I'm not sure what that means exactly, but I never went to school and never had a family like the kids in the village. I don't think I missed having a mum and dad. I didn't think about it much. Sometimes when I was beaten I used to think, I wonder if my dad would have beaten me, but most of the time I just got on with my life. I never get beaten now. Rita and Eric wouldn't allow anyone to beat me.

I used to wonder how the volunteers could bring so much stuff and just give it away to us kids. They also gave stuff to people in the village and to the school. I thought they must live in some magic place where anything they wanted just appeared. That probably meant they had so much they didn't miss what they gave to us.

Not that we kept anything they gave us for long. Whatever the foreign people gave us was always taken away as soon as they left. The staff stole things when no one was looking and threatened to beat us if we told the director because they would have lost their jobs.

The director could have anything she wanted, of course. Once, the English brought a bike for me. It came on a lorry and I was dead quick to learn to ride it. I whizzed through the village – up and down – up and down. Everyone shouted, 'Go, Adrian! Go faster!' I thought I was a king, flying around with the wind making my hair stand up like a cock's comb. But soon it was taken away. Someone said it was sold in the next village. I never had a bike again.

We never had enough food. Someone told me that's why I'm still so skinny. I've never caught up my proper body

108

weight. During the daytime when the cow was grazing I had to hoe the fields and make sure the crops were good for the year. In the summer it was hot as hell – out in the field hoeing, hoeing, hoeing. My back used to ache and I had permanent blisters on my hands. But when I looked at Dorin and I thought, if he can manage, so can I. Working made me strong. I can work for eight hours in the fields without getting tired.

I often get really bad toothache and I've had lots of teeth removed. I can remember when I was in pain for over two months. It kept throbbing and throbbing. I begged the director to let me see a dentist but she told me to bear it like a man. I don't think she wanted to waste money on me. In the end I dug the tooth out with a bit of metal I found and that hurt.

I've made lots of visits to the dentist and it is never good news for me. Rita says the Murgeni dentist is not very clean. I've never noticed really. There isn't a waiting-room. Everybody who needs treating stands in the surgery, leaning against the wall and watching some other poor sod in the chair. Rita says the dentist uses the same instruments for each patient without cleaning them properly. She seems to think that's not very nice. The dentist does wash his hands, from time to time under a cold water tap, but there isn't any soap.

If you want to have a painkilling injection you have to visit the chemist across the road and buy the anaesthetic and also get the syringe and needle. I never had a painkiller until Rita arrived. This is not something many Romanians can afford. Every time he gets hold of me the dentist hurts *me. I haven't got many more teeth to cause any problems, so that's good, isn't it?*

I liked it best if I could drive the camine horse and cart, but that didn't happen often. I always had to fetch the water for the camine as we had no well of our own. The groundsman and me took the horse and cart outside the village to a water hole twice a day. In the winter the hole was frozen and I had to beat it with a stick to break the ice before we could drop the bucket down. We'd fill up milk churns with water and bring them back on the cart. It could be a freezing cold job. I never had any warm clothes and only sandals on my feet. We never had socks till Rita looked after us. Now we wear socks every day and I have three pairs of footwear. I've got wellington boots, trainers and sandals. I forgot – I've got indoor slippers, too.

Sometimes, but not often, cook at the camine would let me stand in the kitchen to get warm. The smell of the soup always made me hungry. I used to like watching her make the bread. Great big loaves that she cooked in the oven over the fire.

Chapter 10

I settled into my job at Eton College quickly and I loved it. The boys in my care were a delight and I enjoyed a privileged lifestyle and had a lot of fun, too. But most importantly, I had school holidays which gave me the opportunity to return to Romania on a regular basis.

My time at College was surreal at times. What became my everyday life was far removed from anything I'd known. And it was a whole world apart from Giurcani.

My Housemaster, James Cook, was a special person and 'tolerated' my huge passion for Romania. He also nurtured me through the pitfalls of college life. My role, in addition to the care of the boys, was a social one within the college: dinner parties, coffee mornings, drinks parties and support for the boys at sporting occasions, including the wonderful fourth of June rowing regatta. I regularly helped James entertain parents and visitors.

Some of the most memorable occasions included an invitation to lunch at Windsor Castle, followed by the Order of the Garter ceremony in the chapel. One of my boys was a page to the Queen and his parents very kindly invited me to join them. Another occasion, when James Cook was less than happy with me, involved a sporting event. Our boys lost in the final of the House rugby. Having shouted support from the sidelines throughout the match I commiserated with them when they came off the field. James heard me tell them, 'Never mind – it's only a game.' He was mightily unimpressed. 'My Dame!' he exclaimed. 'Never has such a sentiment been heard on the playing fields of Eton!'

I lived in a beautiful apartment on the third floor of Walpole House and was responsible for the pastoral care of fifty-two boys and the hiring and daily duties of eight staff. My sitting-room window looked out onto a glorious garden and to Windsor Castle beyond. It felt far removed from Romania.

I was spoiled beyond my wildest dreams. No duster soiled my hands; I had no need to clean a bathroom or shimmy across a carpet with a hoover. Everything was done for me. The house chef cooked for my dinner parties and I had a living allowance and salary of generous proportions. What a bizarre world I inhabited.

****

After a few years of visiting Giurcani I became increasingly disillusioned. Donated items were regularly missing; rooms were grubby and the programmes to get the children walking were patchy, to say the least. It really bothered me. And of course, other disasters had occurred around the world which had redirected fund raising efforts away from Romania.

I tried to help the village school, which needed books, pencils and paper. Such simple things, but the children even had to share their writing books. Some children went to school in the morning and others in the afternoon so that the meagre resources could be shared between them.

One thing I will never forget was the quality of the children's work in that school. Despite a woeful lack of resources, Didi Rotaru imparted his knowledge with huge enthusiasm. I suppose it was an old-fashioned school with the three Rs taught daily, together with geography, history and basic science. The walls displayed maps of the world which I always thought exhibited a certain irony. Exotic countries were shamelessly flaunting themselves before people who had chance to explore their wonders.

Didi didn't need to tell me how difficult life was at school. There were so many things he needed but with typical Romanian patience he was resigned to waiting. He wanted to put a metal fence around the school and playground and this request perplexed me. I thought it was a bizarre way to spend charity money – on fencing. I listened to the reasoning but I had problems in agreeing that fencing should be a high priority. I knew that Romanians are obsessed with fencing in their homes and wondered if this was just a personal desire, rather than a necessity.

Didi explained further: the playground was being used by vagabonds and some local men as an area to drink alcohol and it was often used as a lavatory. He feared for the safety of the children. He also felt that the kindergarten children, in particular, were in danger of running into the road and under a horse and cart. It sounded both unpleasant and dangerous. Didi told me that if the area was fenced he could start projects with the children, including using it for sport in the school holidays and many other things.

I was coming round to the idea. I had always promised myself that I would listen to local views and try never to draw comparisons with life at home. I trusted Didi and if he said it was an important issue, then who was I to disagree? However, the cost of metal fencing around such a large area was phenomenal. I had to get my thinking cap on to find ways to raise the money.

****

I discussed the various problems in Giurcani with my friends at Eton. Four Dames who were particularly interested in my work offered to form a committee to raise money for the project. And so I put my concerns to them about the metal fence request. They could see the advantage of having a secure compound for small children, (some were as young as four years old.) We also agreed that school holiday projects could be a huge success in the village. And so it was decided to make the fence part of our goal, along with books and other resources.

I went to see Poppy Anderson, the wife of the then Headmaster, and shared my aspirations with her. She is a humanitarian lady and listened intently while I poured out my story and, luckily for me, she agreed to help. When people of influence offer support it encourages you to hold on to your dreams. You really believe it can happen. And so it did.

I was introduced by Poppy to the wife of the Provost of Eton, Lady Acland. This set progress in motion in a way I could never have imagined. Jenny Acland is another charitable lady and she, too, offered her help. To this end, she invited me to join an International Ladies Club which she was in the process of setting up at Eton. She explained that when her husband, Sir Anthony, was in post as British Ambassador in the United States during the time of Ronald Reagan, she had created a similar group in Washington.

114

They regularly debated world affairs and gave money to worthy causes. I liked the sound of that.

The group met every other month, each meeting being held at a different venue. The most memorable was the Tower of London in the private apartments overlooking the grounds.

Jenny suggested I should be the speaker at the inaugural meeting to be held at College in the Provost's Lodge. I was terrified. I knew that other members included foreign ambassadors' wives and friends of the Aclands. One other Dame had also been invited to join the membership which gave me some support.

After my talk and slide show to the International Ladies Club I was asked to speak to the Jane Shaw Society which is an historic club for women at Eton. It was after this that I was approached by the women of Eton College who were interested in sending gifts to the women in Giurcani. They asked me to give them guidelines for suitable gifts, which I was very happy to do. I was thrilled with the offer, particularly as I was due to visit the village again for Christmas. As a result of their generosity I took with me an array of small, beautifully-wrapped gifts.

I remember the happy occasion well, as that year I delivered the gifts around Giurcani by horse and cart, kindly arranged by Didi. There was deep snow for my entire visit which made the delivery extra special. For many village women it was not only a surprise to be singled out for a gift, but also the first western gift they had ever received. It was a huge success.

Another outcome of my introduction to Jenny Acland was a grand musical recital which was performed in College Chapel in aid of Guircani. The Eton choir and orchestra rendered an amazing concert of music by Romanian composers. Tickets were sold and both parents and locals supported it. I've never forgotten the feeling of joy when I discovered the number of people who were prepared to support those children. College Chapel was full to bursting.

Angela came up from Kent for the occasion and we were both bubbling with excitement during the whole evening. The talented choir and orchestra filled the chapel with spine-tingling sound and it was moving for me to see the Eton boys, all from privileged backgrounds, playing and singing their hearts out for 'my children.'

Sir Anthony and Lady Acland generously hosted a drinks party after the concert and guests were invited into their beautiful home for wine and canapés. Staff in traditional black and white uniforms moved gracefully among us, never leaving a glass unfilled. A silver chalice had been placed on the vast oak sideboard in the hall and at the end of the evening it was brimming with twenty and fifty-pound notes. I was deeply moved. Close to three thousand pounds was put into the charity bank account the next day. As a result of that evening, I returned to Romania to pay, not only for the fencing Didi so desired, but also winter shoes for the camine children, books and pens for the school and also play equipment for the nursery school in the village.

My small group of supportive Dames met most Saturday lunchtimes at the Pineapple, a local pub. Here we discussed many things, including life at Eton for women, always an interesting topic, and also our fundraising ideas for Romania. (We became known to the Eton boys as 'The Pineapple Dames'.) Apparently we were the first Dames ever to confess to meeting in a pub and also the first to be seen in public wearing jeans. The boys loved it – at last, they said, they had Dames who were proper people! The hierarchy accepted us with outward good grace although I did hear whispers that we were, on occasion, the topic of conversation at certain dinner parties. Eton was in fear of catching up with the twentieth century.

News of our fundraising spread throughout the college and we had a kind offer from the Roman Catholic priest who was an artist of some repute. He had painted two beautiful watercolours of College and Lower Chapel and kindly agreed we could have limited edition prints created from the originals. The idea was to sell them to parents, old boys and associates of the college.

We took a risk. The printing process was expensive and we had no idea how many people would want to buy prints. Spending charity money is always more of a headache than spending your own and we wondered if people associated with the College would prefer to collect original art. However, we decided to go ahead with the idea, trusting that old boys and parents would support us.

A lot of time and care was given to getting the quality right and we were eventually pleased with the 500 limited edition prints. We were lucky. The prints were particularly popular with boys who were leaving school that year and we sold 410, which I believe is considered a good effort in art circles.

The prints raised over five thousand pounds and I was able to put more essential items into the village school in Giurcani. The money provided paint to improve the interior of the classrooms, a new floor in the entrance lobby and a couple of new windows. It also kept the bank balance healthy.

Later that year some of the senior boys in my house decided to raise money for me at the Eton Summer Fair. I had a quantity of tea-towels printed with drawings done by some of the camine children. Angela and I had asked the children to 'draw themselves' on our second visit and the resulting work of art was turned into yet another money-making tool. The boys gamely sold tea-towels at the Fair, their enthusiasm reminiscent of barrow boys in the East End of London. More money came our way.

The Eton boys showed great interest in the Romanian project and often came to my apartment to look at the most recent photos and chat about progress. Unexpectedly, in 1992, three of the senior boys asked me about the possibility of volunteering in Romania for a short time during their coming gap year. I thought it would be great. Didi arranged for them to teach English in both the primary school in Giurcani and also the secondary school in the nearby village of Pecan. The boys would stay in his home for which they would pay board and lodging.

I remember how impressed Didi was to learn that one of the boys he'd be hosting was a godchild of Prince

Charles and also the nephew of Camilla. This visit took place just after the high profile press offensive on Charles and Camilla went viral. Another boy on his way to Giurcani was the child of a very famous family who own a private bank. But Romania is a great leveller and the minute they arrived we were all equals.

The boys travelled out with me when their exams finished and stayed on after I returned. I have some very fond memories of those weeks: Eton boys washing their underwear in a bowl of water in the back garden, their first introduction to life in the village, and also the joy of watching how easily they slipped into a game of football with the older camine boys. I have a photo of an Etonian shaving Adrian with a new, whizzy razor. The razor was, of course, given to Adrian for future use.

I'd like to say the Eton boys were impeccably behaved while in Romania, but sadly not. I learnt, to my horror that one boy thought it would be a joke to feed laxatives to the family pig which killed it in a particularly horrid way. That dead pig was a massive loss to the family who relied on it for food that year.

But the hiccups didn't prevent me allowing four more boys to travel out to Romania the following year. This time, they were presented with a strict list of what was expected from them. I must say the second group were better behaved.

****

In 1994 an old relationship of mine with a police officer called Eric Trotman from Gloucestershire was fanned back into flames and turned into something permanent. It may sound dramatic to say he was the love of my life, but it was the truth. I had been in love with Eric for over twenty years although it never looked as if we would have the opportunity to be together. So I had got on with my own life. But at last, surprisingly, we had our chance to be happy.

I decided I would leave my job at Eton and return to my routes in Gloucestershire. Eric and I were touched when the school Chaplain offered to marry us in College Chapel but it was an offer we decided not to accept. I was sad in many ways to be leaving Eton, but a whole new life lay ahead of me, so how could I harbour regret? Eton and her people were superbly generous to my project in Romania and also to me. I loved my years on your hallowed ground.

Thank you, Eton College.

Chapter 11

Dorin

Once I learnt to walk I was given duties every day. The director went easy on me at first, asking only that I helped to serve the meals or make her coffee and bring it to the office. But after a while I was sent out to hoe the fields with Adrian, Dan and Gheorgie and this was really hard. When you don't have hands or feet, it's not easy to hold a hoe.

I found a way to feed myself which involves holding a spoon in both my fingers and swinging it from the plate to my mouth. In the early days, when I was learning, I was pretty slow and most days some kid took food from me. I soon learned to speed up and now I'm ace at it. Rita says I'm liked greased lightning with a spoon and fork. It's much the same with farm tools. You just adapt and find a way. Now we've got our own land to look after I always do my share. I'm as good at hoeing as Adrian or Gheorgie. I never think about not having hands or feet these days.

When I was a kid I wasted a lot of energy feeling sorry for myself. Later, when I worked out how to deal with life, I learned to stand my ground, find a way to get what I needed to survive and then things weren't so bad.

One year Rita took lots of photos of my hands and feet to take back to England. She said she would see if there was a doctor who could help. I didn't think it would happen, though. I told her that I was not going to have my feet cut off and I made her promise me she would never let that happen. The next year she told me that she had tried but nothing could be done. I wasn't disappointed 'cos I knew it would never happen.

****

Gheorgie
One day they came and took me away. Guircani wasn't much of a place to leave but I was sad. I had friends there and no one told me where I was going. Um...it rained that day, I remember because I'd put my wellington boots on in the morning to take out the rubbish and the shitty bed sheets from room 6.

Mostly there were two kids in every bed so I used to wait until they both had a crap and then I only had to change the sheets once. Viorel, who worked in the laundry and had the job of taking the turds out of the bedding, was grateful, too.

Well, those wellington boots never went with me. The director took them off me and told me to walk in the mud in my plastic sandals. Can you believe that? She said the new place could provide me with footwear and I wasn't taking hers.

I travelled in a white van sent by the Direction for the Protection of Children in Vaslui. I remember another kid went with me, but I didn't like her. She was crazy and tried to steal everybody's food which she stored in her knickers. Even when she had her monthlies. Nobody wanted to steal it back then. She was a screamer at night and she used to give me headaches. I often get headaches you know. You'd have thought she was being eaten by wolves some nights. The staff said it was nightmares but nobody cared. Adrian used to hit her and tell her to shut up. If she took no notice,

Ionelle used to threaten to stick his thing in her ass. That usually did the trick. Anyway, that day we were bundled into the van and I never said goodbye to anybody. Adrian was out with the cow and I don't know where Dorin was.

They took me to Husi, which is a place for handicapped people. I don't know how old I was, but I knew I wasn't a kid any more. And I knew I was handicapped, but not mad. Most of them in Husi are mad.

When we arrived I was taken up to the second floor and we passed two women running naked down the stairs. They were being chased by a very cross bloke who was yelling at them and threatening to tie them to their bed for a week if they didn't come back. I felt afraid. They didn't stop and I could see them out in the garden from the high up window. They were screaming as if they were about to die.

I hated it at Husi. The staff were worse than the ones in Guircani. At least some of the women there were nice to you if you did exactly as you were told and worked hard. But in Husi it was really bad. I first had to share a bed with a skinny bloke who kept shouting in his sleep and kept me awake for nights. He used to wave his thing at me and ask me to do horrible things to it. Eventually the staff changed him for an old bloke who snored and sometimes peed the bed. I would wake in the morning soaked in his pee. It wasn't nice.

I was given a job washing the floors. Not just in my room but all the rooms on the second floor. I had to carry buckets of water upstairs after fetching them from the water tap on the ground floor. The tap on our floor never worked and was never mended in the whole time I was there. They made me put some liquid stuff in the water which they told me was to stop fleas. It smelled disgusting and it made the skin on my hands come off. It was hard work washing floors all day. As soon as you thought you'd finished, some bloke would have a crap in the corner of one of the rooms and I'd have to start again. If he'd smeared it on his skin, more often than not I'd be made to clean him up, too. I used the water from my bucket 'cos I couldn't be bothered to go all the way back down for clean water. Not to wash a bloke who would do it all again tomorrow.

They make you wear clothes with numbers on in Husi. I was in Room 11 so I was only allowed to wear clothes with an 11 on. I could recognise an 11 easily but often the best clothes were grabbed by other blokes. I've never been one to push in a queue. In the winter there were never enough warm clothes. I needed warm clothes 'cos I had to keep going to get water, but no one listened. I was always cold and my feet were always soaking wet from the water I carried. I hated that place. I missed the animals in Guircani and Dorin. Adrian was my friend, too. I like working with animals but I didn't like cleaning floors.

One day I was told to undress and leave my clothes on the bed. They gave me an old dressing-gown to put on and it had no tie so I was embarrassed when my privates poked out.

Nobody said why I had to take my clothes off. I wondered if I had to see the doctor. I had told the women for weeks that I had sore eyes. Perhaps, I thought, at last I would get some medicine for them.

124

Eventually I was pushed into a transport van with six other fellows and we were taken to another camine. I still have sore eyes all these years later, even though I can have medicine now. Rita makes sure we have money for my eye drops. They told me at the hospital in Birlad that the damage is forever 'cos nobody listened to me when I was younger. Nobody ever listened to me in the old days. I hope I don't go blind when I'm old.

Chapter 12

While I was at Eton my adoptive father died and I was now the owner of the house in Gloucestershire where I'd lived for part of my childhood. As Eric lived in Gloucestershire too, it was to my family home that I returned after saying goodbye to Eton College.

Eric and I were planning to get married the following year and I was quick to introduce him to the Isles of Scilly, a place he'd never been. He was as enchanted as most people who visit.

My life was wonderful. I was in the flush of wedding preparations and my sons were living close by. They were both working and Robert had a charming girlfriend in Bath. I hoped the relationship would develop in the direction of marriage and, some while later we welcomed Katherine to the family. Eric's two children were generous in their acceptance of me and so we had four wonderful children between us.

After our wedding in the tiny church in Cherington, we spent another year in Gloucestershire waiting for Eric to complete his thirty years service in the police force. We talked a lot about our future plans. At forty-nine Eric felt too young to retire and was keen for us to have a business together.

One day, out of the blue, he asked if I would consider going back to live in Scilly. I was surprised, particularly as he'd only visited the islands a couple of times and for relatively short periods. However, I took little persuading and so, after looking at our joint finances, we decided we could afford to house-hunt on St. Mary's.

We bought a house in 1998 at Old Town with the intention of turning it into a guest house. It was a stone-built, Victorian house situated right on Old Town Bay and the views from the house and garden are breath-taking – you can almost touch the sea. The downside was the amount of work to be done to turn it into a business establishment.

The house needed gutting from roof to foundations, but it wasn't all bad news. We could just afford to do the work, although it would be a combination of hard labour by us and specialist help as needed. Luckily, there was a separate cottage attached at the back which was in good repair. We could live there while we did the work and then turn the cottage into a self-catering holiday let when the main business was up and running.

It was a happy time for us. Newly married and with a common goal, we put our heart and soul into Tolman House. Every morning we woke to the sound of the tide, sometimes a gentle lap of water on sand and often a heavy heartbeat of foaming spray thrown metres high over Pulpit Rock.

During this busy time I didn't visit Romania. It was the longest period of time that I'd not returned to the village but it was never far from my thoughts. I made occasional telephone calls to Didi, but gleaned little information about the camine.

One day, in 1999, when we had finished the renovation of our guest house and our B&B business was growing, we received a telephone call from Jan Broeders in Holland. He told me that he had visited Romania and found time to call into the camine at Giurcani. He apologised that he had bad news, but he felt sure that I would want to know. He'd found the children hungry, badly clothed and lacking medication. He said the camine was filthy again, but the most urgent concern was the children's desperate need of food. The director told him that money was short; her food budget was half of what was needed. I could imagine her lack of concern and Gaelic shrug – what could she do about it?

I was deeply distressed. My mind filled with images of all those children – each one known by name. How could this have happened again? And I felt guilty. I'd been so busy with my own life that I'd failed them. I had to go back.

****

Eric

When I first visited Romania, if I'm honest, it was just to please Rita. I knew her passion and commitment to the boys was a lifetime thing and it was a case of 'join the party or be a wallflower'. We got married after a long wait to be together and I knew that Romania was a big part of her life. I'm sure neither of us realised just how big it would become and I didn't feel indifferent for long. Soon I was sucked up by the depth and breadth of the cause.

My first visit was in 1999. Suddenly, the camine and all the deprivation I'd heard about was right before my eyes. And nothing prepares you for what you see, hear and smell. Even after thirty years as a policeman it still shook me to the core. And this was happening in Europe.

When we arrived in Bucharest I remember thinking it looked like an up-and-coming city. OK, it had areas of deprivation and there were beggars on the streets, but nothing was very different from a dozen other European cities.

I knew the journey to Guircani was not an easy one. Seven hours on a train with the hope that someone would be in Birlad to meet us. But nothing deters my wife and Rita's excitement was palpable. Every time she visits, I was to learn, she gets an excitement in the pit of her stomach and every time she leaves she gets tearful. I have to say that these days, since we have managed to give the boys their own house, she leaves with a lighter heart. But when she left those pathetic little kids in the camine to the mercy of the staff and, ultimately, the authorities, she used to feel a deep grief that rose up and almost choked her. I tried various ways to prevent the massive upset when it was time to go home, but nothing worked. I just steeled myself to watch the lady I love turn herself inside out with grief for 'her kids.'

****

Eric and I flew to Romania. For me it was a journey filled with more than the usual trepidation. What would we find? For Eric it was different. I knew that despite all the stories he'd heard over the years he was concerned about coping with village life. Would he take to kids with disabilities? Was he ready for filth and hunger, to say nothing of the living conditions he'd heard about in graphic detail? For him it was a step into the unknown, well outside his comfort zone as a police officer.

On this trip we flew to Bucharest from Heathrow. Jan Broeders had arranged for us to be met at the airport by the manager of the Joseph Foundation which carried out humanitarian work in the city of Iasi. This jolly man took us by car from the airport and we spent a night at the Foundation house. Staff would help us hire a rental car to get to Giurcani the next day.

It was here that we first met Daniela Cornestean who worked at the Foundation as a psychologist. We stayed in her office on a bed sofa that first night and awoke the next morning to a hoar frost sparkling on the cabbages outside our window. I remember we overslept and Daniela, who was waiting to start work, was too polite to knock!

We met not only Daniela but also Mara, the social worker. Both women gave us a guided tour of the house, introduced us to the children and also the work they were doing. They explained how they organised the fostering and adoption programme for the babies in their care, including all the court paper work and the challenge of Romanian red tape. Many of the children were due to be adopted into families in other European countries.

The house was full of happy, healthy, smiling children. And it was so clean! Young babies, children who went to school daily and even teenagers were having their lives turned around by the dedicated staff. This was a Christian organisation and received money from churches and individuals all over Europe.

The Joseph Foundation was licensed by the Romanian Government to arrange adoptions both inside and outside Romania. It was usually the babies who were brought to the Foundation straight from the streets who attracted early adoption. All were cared for and loved during those waiting months and the prospective parents visited as regularly as they were able. When the processes were completed they took their precious, adopted child away to a new life.

Another aspect of Daniela's work was a programme with street children. The Foundation took in children in difficulty, found mainly through soup-kitchens on the streets. They helped either to reunite them with their families, after counselling, or kept them at the Foundation home and ensured they went to school. A programme of working with gypsy children and many other worthwhile projects were also undertaken by a devoted staff who were paid very little money. It was an inspirational place.

Daniela worked on a one-to-one basis with some of the most disturbed children, many of whom had been sexually abused. She also arranged holidays for them in the countryside, Christmas parties and many things to make them feel loved for the first time in their lives.

Sadly, foreign adoption was stopped by the Romanian Government about three years after that visit. An English woman was filmed 'buying' a baby from gypsies and this attracted a lot of television coverage. Now life got really tough for the Foundation as it relied upon generous, prospective parents to keep the house running

Without Daniela we would never have managed to release our three boys from the State system. She also facilitated buying the house for them to live in. Apart from all that, we have grown to love her. She has visited us in

Scilly and Devon and also at our holiday home in Spain. We have visited her family in Sighet, an area of Romania near the Hungarian border. She comes from a loving home and her parents are immensely proud of her. Luckily for us, Daniela has near perfect English and this makes our lives so much easier, particularly when legal matters had to be resolved. It also made me lazy with my spoken Romanian!

The work at the Joseph Foundation in Iasi was an eye-opener for us. Here, Romanians were working with children to the same standard as the Dutch Red Cross which was influenced by Jan Broeders. Much of the Foundation's funding was raised by Jan in Holland and also from the generosity of foreign parents, many of whom stayed in touch with the staff and sent photos of the children growing up. We would return many times to the Foundation, but the next day we said our farewells and set out in our rented car for Giurcani.

****

The only people in Giurcani with whom we could discuss our concerns about the children at the camine were Didi and Tori Rotaru. Our arrival was met with huge enthusiasm, especially for Eric who was told 'It's about time someone looked after Rita.'

I hoped our friends would know about the feeding problems at the camine as I felt sure that gossip would be rife around the village. And I was right. After conversations late into the night we discovered that, not only was the camine suffering, but the whole country was in dire straits. As the camines were at the bottom of the government pecking order, this was where the most radical cost-cutting had fallen. It was as grim as I'd feared.

Eric and I visited the camine the next day and I was overjoyed to meet Dorin and Adrian who were waiting at the gates for us. Word had spread of our arrival. Most of the well known faces were still at the camine and I took Eric on a tour of the salons to meet them. Many of the women gave us hugs and told me of their fears for the future. They agreed that standards had slipped, but said not only the camine kids were hungry but also their own families. They had no money, they explained.

The children were indeed a sorry sight, but on reflection, they hadn't reverted to the really bad old days of 1991. But they were far from fine. Many of them had skin complaints and weeping sores on their faces. Some had hacking coughs. They were all thin and poorly dressed and very few had smiles. Malnutrition was again on the march. But for me, a great sadness was the absence of Gheorgie. He had been sent to an adult institution.

The Director greeted us in her office with cool hospitality. She was actually warmer to Eric than to me. We had a gift of coffee for her to sweeten the meeting and for about ten minutes we played around with niceties. But I wasn't in the mood for small talk. I asked the director for her view of the current situation. Was she having difficulties feeding and clothing the children? Were the staff receiving their salaries? She answered with a shrug and a 'what can I do' attitude.

The staff had received no wages for three months and there was very little food for the children, she told me. I asked her why the children were so poorly dressed and clearly in need of medicines. How was she managing; what was she most in need of? When I'd left two years before, there had been huge piles of clothes stacked in the store room. They'd been sent from England by road and should have lasted for three or four years. She allowed us to look in the store room which was empty. We took our leave with heavy hearts.

Eric and I felt we could raise money to help feed the children in the camine, but our worry was how to administer the programme. The problem for me was a lack of trust in the camine director and the government bodies. I had witnessed too many shady goings-on to have any confidence that our money would be used appropriately. It was unthinkable that I would trust either with the large sums required.

Didi had a good idea. His son Dragoş had a friend with a car, a rare commodity at that time, and they made an offer we couldn't refuse. It was arranged that once every month Dragoş would go to Birlad to buy food in bulk and deliver it to the camine to feed the children. We devised a list of essentials to be purchased and I went to discuss the plan with the director. She agreed the list was appropriate, adding one or two other items that she needed. On our insistence, a paperwork trail of the purchases would be created for our inspection. We then had to leave it to those we trusted most.

To add to our worries, there was talk around the village that the camine might close some time in the not too distant future. The oldest children would be sent to adult institutions, we were told, and foster homes would be found for the younger ones. This time we felt it was serious. The European Union had stipulated that Romania needed to 'clean up the orphanages' if their bid to join was to have any chance of success. This set alarm bells ringing for me. Did this mean, at last, that all the older boys would end up in Husi?

The boys were worried, too. The grapevine was working and they had obviously been talking about it between themselves. Eventually three of them came to us with a request. But what an enormous request it was. They asked if we could help them have a little house of their own in the village. Somewhere they could lead independent lives.

Adrian told me he was 'sick of all the screaming kids in the camine and being hungry.' He wanted to live a proper life with his friends. I have to say it came as a shock, although, looking back, I have no idea why. Why had it never crossed my mind to create an Independent Living Project for the more able boys?

Eric and I gave them no more hope than that we would think about it. We both realised what a huge undertaking it would be. And a life-long commitment too. Eric says that he knew in that instant that somehow we would find a way to do it. He said it was 'written all over my face.' I can't comment about that!

Adrian
I ran away once. I don't know which year exactly but it was a time when things were shit at the camine. Even worse

than usual. I remember we'd had an inspection. A smart car came up the drive with three men and a woman in it. It was a rainy day and only the biggest kids were outside, those who had work to do. The visitors were smartly dressed and didn't look at any of us kids.

The woman got out first and picked her way over the mud in spike-heel shoes, looking at the ground as if it was out to get her. The three men marched towards the office just as the director came out to meet them. I knew one of the men 'cos he'd called at the camine lots of times. I knew they were all from the Protection of Children in Vaslui 'cos I know most things that go on in the camine. They were in the office for hours and all the staff stopped work to discuss what they might be there for.

There were several ideas. Violetta thought they might be going to close us down but no one else agreed with her. Nina thought they were going to give everyone a wage increase but she got laughed at. 'Not a chance was what most people thought about that. Dorin suggested we were all going to have to work harder and Bianca clipped him hard around the ears. He just laughed and told them they wouldn't think they were so clever when he was proved right.

Eventually the director came out of the office with a very grim face and the visitors disappeared without another word. I knew there was trouble coming, but nothing was said that day. The director went home early after shouting instructions to the staff to get back to work.

The next day all hell let loose. Apparently the bigwigs from Vaslui had told the director that their accounts showed someone was stealing food from the camine. They said that the daily allowance for the children would be cut by some huge amount until further notice. The thief must be found and sacked. They also said that three women must be laid off and the others must work harder.

How Dorin crowed! He talked about it for days, telling the women that he knew everything, even before it happened. But the worst news of all was that the four oldest boys, and that included me, were to be sent to Husi. That's an institute for adults and the worst place on earth. Ever since I can remember I've been told about Husi and I would rather die than go there. The director was particularly cross about that because I did a lot of work for her. Not only on the camine farm but I used to work her land for her and sweep the paths and clean her house. I also used to pick her grapes and make wine in the autumn.

I spoke to Dan and Dorin about it and told them I was going to run away. They didn't agree with me and said I wouldn't dare to do it. So I made my plans on my own, carefully saving bits of bread to help with my hunger when I got on the road.

I knew that I needed the weather to be dry if I was to have a chance to survive. I decided I would hang on the back of a hay cart leaving the village and when we got to Murgeni I would start walking to Birlad. Once I reached Birlad I thought I would find a way to sneak onto a train going to Bucharest or anywhere, really. I'd heard that in Bucharest kids lived in the underground sewers and they all looked after each other. That sounded good.

When you can't read it's hard to work out things like where a train is going, but I was going to have a good try. To be honest, I didn't care where I went, just so long as it wasn't Husi. After about three days I'd saved some bread, I had a bottle of water and an apple I'd nicked from the kitchen. The plan was to leave in the daytime as we're all locked in at night. I knew I'd have to do my chores first or I'd be missed and they would start looking for me. As it turned out, I showed up for tea to have one last meal before I went. I told Dan I was leaving and asked him two things; cover for me that evening when I should have been working with the animals and please don't tell Dorin 'cos he can't keep his mouth shut.

A lot of the carts come through the village from Gagesti. They are mostly on their way to Murgeni but usually stop in Guircani so that the men can drink beer at the pub. I hung around waiting for a cart with a load big enough for me to hide in. Eventually a bloke drove his horse down the street and he had a kid sitting beside him, I guessed he was about eight or nine. The cart was full of cabbages and a bit of hay. They disappeared into the pub to order their drinks. I didn't have much time 'cos I knew they would come back outside to drink them, so I dived into the cart and covered myself with cabbages.

There was an old coat on the top of the load and I managed to cover myself well. I didn't think anyone would see me. After about half an hour I heard the shouts of goodbye and within a minute we were rumbling towards Murgeni. My heart was bumping hard.

It felt like it took forever to get to Murgeni but I spent the time working out how I would get off the cart without being seen. I knew I couldn't wait until we were right in the town as someone could spot me the minute I jumped out. Instead, I decided to roll off the back of the cart just before we got to the town and then I could start the long walk to Birlad.

I'd been to Birlad twice before, both times to the hospital. I knew it was a really long way and would probably take me all night. I sneaked a couple of looks out from under the cabbages and thought I recognised the church on the outskirts of Murgeni. I was on my way. This was my moment. I rolled as quietly as I could off the back of the cart, taking two cabbages with me, and I kept rolling until I was in the ditch on the side of the road. It's really a water gully that channels the rainwater in the winter months. All the roads in Romania have them. I'd decided to hide there in case the driver heard the bump and looked back to check his load. I'll never know if he did but I was free, even if I was covered in dust and clutching two cabbages as if my life depended on them. I hoped I'd be able to sell them for a few lei to help me on my way.

Now the long walk began. I'd seen people on the side of the roads trying to wave cars down, wanting to hitch a ride. But at first I was too scared in case someone from Giurcani was driving. We only had three cars in the village 'cos only the richest people could afford them, but I couldn't risk being recognised. So I walked. I thought about all the things I would do with my life now that I was free of the camine and none of it included work. I had done enough work to last a lifetime.

A couple of carts passed me and the men didn't even say hello. Then an empty cart came along really slowly 'cos the horse was lame and the man asked me where I was going. I told him I needed to get to Birlad and he said I could hop on but he was only going three miles up the road. We chatted for a bit and I told him I was going to visit my family. I think he believed me. When we reached his house I asked if he wanted to buy the cabbages but he said he already had loads in his garden. He said, 'Good luck,' and I started walking again.

It wasn't long before a car stopped. A man put his window down and asked if I wanted a lift. I'd never seen him before and I knew he didn't live in Giurcani so I said, 'Thanks.' I'd never ridden in the front of a car before. I felt like a king. I told the bloke the same story about my family in Birlad but he didn't show much interest. He had a bottle of wine tucked down by his feet and he swigged it every now and then as we drove along.

Suddenly the man offered me a drink and asked if I'd eaten anything that day. I lied and said, 'No'. He said he knew a place where we could stop and he'd share some bread and cheese with me. He said he might buy my cabbages too, which made me happy. I took a couple of swigs of his wine when he offered it although it was sour. But I didn't care and I drank it like a man. At last, I thought, I was starting to live like a real person. I was no longer a stupid kid from a camine.

After a while he drove off the main road and stopped in a place in the forest. I thought about the time when I'd had to ask the hospital van to stop so that I could have a pee behind a tree. Now it was nearly dark and it looked a bit frightening. All the trees looked scary and I was beginning to wonder when I would get to Birlad. He said he needed a pee and jumped out so I followed, thinking a pee would be a good idea before I got to Birlad. The wind was blowing through the trees and I couldn't see any moon that night. Just dark, grey sky. I could see his shadow and moved away from him to pee. It seemed polite.

When we got back in the car I noticed he hadn't done up his trousers. He saw me looking and he laughed at me. 'Got any idea what you're going to do next?' he asked. I had. I knew exactly and I realised what a fool I'd been. I was in the middle of nowhere and had no one who was going to help me. The only thing I could think of was to run. I'm a fast runner and he looked a bit porky, to be honest. I was quick. Dead quick, and it was just a second before I was out of his car and running like a rabbit. I darted about to miss the trees which loomed ahead in the darkness. I thought I was running in the direction of the road and this bothered me in case he chased after me. I had to do some quick thinking so I leaped up the nearest tree and sat in the branches with my heart beating so hard I thought it would pop out of my body. I heard him start the car after a while. He probably knew he couldn't run as fast as me but I didn't feel safe until I saw the lights disappear. I'd lost my water and the apple, but I didn't care.

I decided to stay where I was until morning. I wasn't sure if there might be wolves around. I've never seen one but they live in Romanian forests and I didn't want to take any chances. It wasn't a comfortable night. The branch felt strong enough but I was afraid to move much in case my weight made it break and perhaps I would end up with broken bones. So I sat still and tried to think what I would do in the morning. The worst thing was when I remembered my two cabbages were still in his car. So much for selling them. Still, I was used to having nothing. I'd have to beg for food.

I saw the morning light coming up from my perch in the tree and had a bit of a chuckle at myself. What the hell had I done? I thought about Dan and Dorin having some tea and bread for breakfast and my stomach rumbled. I decided to risk getting down and tried to find my way back to the road. I didn't recognise anything so I had to make my best guess. After a while I heard the sound of traffic and headed towards it. I decided to walk to Birlad and I'd definitely refuse any offers of a lift. I knew what some men were like. I'd had enough things done to me to last a lifetime. I didn't feel very safe.

When I found the road I started to walk. Quite fast, even though I was starving. I told myself that I would never be free if I wasn't brave and hunger wasn't going to stop me. I must have walked for over an hour when a car stopped beside me. I refused to look at the driver and kept walking. Then a woman's voice shouted my name. Oh God! It was the director and her husband. She was out of the car and catching me up. She screamed, 'Where the hell have you been?' And then, 'You little fool.' I eventually looked at *her as she grabbed my arm and pulled me into the car. I gave in. I knew when I was beaten. In fact, beaten is probably what I was going to be. But the worst bit about the whole thing was that I had started walking the wrong way. I was walking back to Giurcani and would never have made it to Birlad. People are right. I am stupid. And I thought I was on my way to Husi for sure.*

Chapter 13

And so Eric and I returned home with two projects instead of one. We needed to find a way to provide food for the camine and to purchase a house for the boys. Together they would take a huge amount of money. We had some funds we could use towards the food campaign already in the charity account, but as it was an open-ended effort we had no idea how much money we needed. Money for the house would have to be raised.

When we went home to Scilly we decided to approach two groups of local people – the Methodist Church, of which I was a member and The Rotary Club to which Eric belonged. We offered to give each organisation a talk, showing them slides about our work. They both promptly arranged dates and together Eric and I shared our hopes with everyone, not only for the hungry children, but also those three boys and their desire to have a house of their own. And the response was amazing. With great generosity, people supported us.

The fundraising began in earnest. We organised strawberry teas and jazz in our garden at Tolman House, concerts, suppers, sponsored walks and many other things – all done with huge amounts of love and enthusiasm from caring people. A black tie ball also brought in much-needed funds.

The island community and visitors alike became involved and gave to the project. It was a humbling experience to receive money given with so much faith. I felt moved that everyone trusted us to do the right thing for those children. And so we did.

Both projects fired people's imagination. Hungry children will soften the hardest hearts and, apart from money, we also had offers of clothes and toys. Many people told us they supported us because we were doing the work ourselves. It was interesting to hear some views about the larger, well known charities; many felt that the bigger charities spend too much money on administration. For our small effort, every penny raised went to the kids.

The arrangement for Didi to receive a regular amount of money was quickly put in place and soon Dragoş was buying and delivering the essential foods for the camine. The list included flour, milk powder, eggs, butter, sugar, cheese, honey from Didi, chicken and yeast. It was agreed that items could be varied should the director make a request that was reasonable. All the paperwork would be kept for our inspection. We knew the system wasn't foolproof but it was the best we could do from a distance. We had trust in the Rotaru family and we continued this aid programme for ten months.

With the food project underway and the continued generosity of the island community and the many visitors, we eventually decided that buying the house was a reality. We contacted Didi and asked if he could find a suitable house for us and also think about who might make suitable 'guardians' for the boys. We asked him not to tell the lads about our decision at that stage.

Around this time Eric and I decided it was time to formalise the fundraising. We were, at times, holding substantial amounts of money in a charity account but felt the time had come to account for it on a more formal basis. And so we applied for charity status from the Charity Commission.

We decided to call the charity the Joseph Foundation and there were two reasons for our choice of name. Daniela's employers, The Joseph Foundation in Iasi, had agreed to have the house bought in their name, (as foreigners were not, at that time, allowed to buy land in Romania;) also, we hoped at some time in the future to give support to Daniela's work, too. We felt it created a sister organisation.

We were delighted to be given Charity Commission status for the Joseph Foundation in the UK.

Chapter 14

Eric and I visited Giurcani again during the summer of 2000. We needed to check on the feeding programme and also to find out what the future held for the camine. My fears were as real as ever that the boys could have been moved away. Also, we felt we needed to make preparation for the Independent Living Scheme Programme if our plans were to come to fruition.

Daniela was very supportive of that particular project and had experience of placing camine children in caring homes. She said she would meet us in the village on our arrival and spend time with a group of boys, assessing them and helping us decide which ones were suitable for independent living. Her own job with the city of Iasi street children brought a wealth of knowledge to the project and we were grateful she was prepared to share it with us. We were anxious to make the right choices to ensure our plans had a real chance of success.

Adrian and Dorin were our first choice of boys to take out of the camine. They were well known to us, hard workers and desperate to make a new life for themselves. They had, in my opinion, all the qualities to ensure success. Although Gheorgie was lost and causing me much heart-ache, Eric persuaded me to focus on the children who were still in the camine.

Among the many we considered was Dan, a tall, well-built lad who was always keen to work. He was a very capable boy but, as with all the others, had never been to school. On a previous visit to the village, Didi, Eric and I had taken him to visit a shoe factory in a nearby town to watch the process of shoe manufacturing. The owners had kindly given him needles, thread and leather to help him get a small business started in the camine. He taught himself to repair shoes and boots and the small amount he charged the villagers made him some pocket money. We thought he deserved to join the project.

I was keen to assess a girl called Luçica. She was about seventeen when she helped me during my first year at the camine and during that long, hot summer she had joined me daily in the salon of children who were bottle fed. I taught her to wash and feed the children and she became adept at caring for their needs.

One day, a small boy had appeared in a cot next to the window. He was able to walk, wasn't undernourished and clearly didn't fit into the regime I was setting up. But Luçica was persistent. She really wanted 'little Adrian' to live in that room and I could think of no reason to refuse her.

And the newest addition was a joy. Instead of sad, sullen eyes from skinny little faces, he was always smiling. We potty-trained him – success created much cheering and clapping – and introduced him to structured play. But I noticed Luçica rarely allowed him far from her side and he obeyed her every instruction. I began to wonder if she was his mother, but when I questioned the staff I was assured that was not the case. They told me she thought he was her little brother and had insisted he be known as 'little Adrian.'

It could be expected that I was unshockable after so many years working around those deprived children. However, very recently that same little boy, now a strapping twenty-five-year-old known as Petico, told me that not only did he know Luçica was his mother but he also knew who his father was. Luçica had been raped by a village man who had acknowledged, in recent years, that Petico was his offspring. Apparently Luçica had been sent to Husi when she was pregnant and returned after the birth. Petico was returned some time later. Luçica remains in Husi today as it was sadly agreed she was unlikely to fit into the project.

And so we all sat down with the three lads and discussed how the project might work. Their enthusiasm was a joy to watch but it was clear they would need 'guardians' to oversee their welfare. Daniela was anxious that our lads would be safe and not taken advantage of by those unsupportive of our aims. She told us that in her view, such things as ensuring they took their medication (Adrian is epileptic) learning to care for their home and managing finances was probably not within their capabilities without support. And of course, they couldn't read or write.

Eric and I also had concerns about the villagers' attitude to our plans. To the best of our knowledge this was a ground-breaking proposal and even today, we have never met anyone who is running a similar project. And this has a down-side. There was a possibility the boys could be treated unkindly or lose their possessions so we definitely needed the right people to oversee their well-being. There were so many issues to consider.

The boys liked Daniela. Her vast experience of working with street kids made her the perfect choice to assess their ability. She'd gained their confidence and they had an excellent rapport. After a few days she came up with her detailed assessment. In her view, Dan would be the leader of any group as he had the highest IQ. Dorin, despite his physical difficulties, was bright and Daniela believed that he would offer much to the project. For Adrian, her views were no surprise to me. He has severe learning difficulties, but is very compliant and a hard worker. For me, Adrian's inclusion was non-negotiable.

Another advantage we took account of was the closeness of the lads; they had grown up like brothers and had weathered many storms together. Several other boys were also considered, but we agreed that they would find it hard to cope without the confines of institutional life, such as it was. Most had difficulties too severe to manage living independently.

The second evening of our deliberations we received a bombshell. Didi told us he had something to say that could seriously affect our plans. He'd been undecided, he said, whether to reveal the news but felt he must. It had come to light that Dan had recently been cautioned by police for making sexual advances to young girls in the village. He had also exposed himself to a camine worker. This news was a major blow for us.

We talked long into the night and agreed that any chance the villagers had to condemn our plans would lower our chances of success. Few were happy that camine boys were going to live amongst them and they would particularly object to a boy with sexual inclinations towards young village girls. This I could understand but there were, of course, also the old prejudices against camine children rearing their heads. But we now had a very real new one.

We couldn't ignore the facts. Daniela had earlier expressed some concerns over Dan's desire to find his family. Unlike the other boys, he was convinced that if he could find his parents they would welcome him home with open arms. We all suspected that was unlikely and Daniela spent time counselling Dan on the matter. Did this mean he would leave the project to search for his roots? I really didn't want the project to start off with major problems and we knew that, whatever the facts of the matter, in the future the 'English' would be blamed for any problems with Dan.

The accusations about him were confirmed by camine staff and within a few days Dan was sent to Husi. I felt bereft. I'd let him down. We heard later that he gained employment with the shoe manufacturer. This was a grain of comfort to offset the conditions in which he lived. Later, he disappeared, presumably to find his family. I still think of him often and pray he found somewhere safe to live.

It was decided that we needed to discuss our project plans with the director of the camine the next day. We knew it would be hard to keep things under wraps once the house was purchased and we would, obviously, need her support for removing the boys from State care. We expected this to be tricky but hoped for some co-operation.

Surely anyone would want the boys to have a better life, particularly boys she had known for more than twenty years? Daniela offered to come as translator and to ensure there could be no misunderstandings.

It was an interesting meeting. We noticed a distinct shift in attitude from the director when faced with Daniela. Maybe it was recognition of her qualifications (all qualifications hold sway in Romania,) or maybe she was embarrassed by the state of her camine before another professional. Who knows? The outcome was a stern warning from her (to me directly) that 'you'll never manage it; and even if you do the villagers will never accept the boys.' We were not deterred by her negativity but we asked her not to discuss our plans with the boys until we were on firmer ground. Of course, she did. She told them, 'Rita will take you into a house but after a couple of years she will forget you. You will have to live on the street when you can't pay your bills.'

We had already made an appointment in Vaslui to meet with the Director for the Protection of Children to discuss what we planned to do. We needed to know the legal implications and if the authorities would put obstacles in our way. We had no expectation that this would be easy either and set off nervously for our meeting in Vaslui.

Daniela was dressed in clothes we called her 'Miss Psychologist' outfit; black skirt, white blouse and high-heeled shoes and she explained the etiquette of such a meeting to us. It appeared to be less straightforward than it would be at home. For a start, we had to buy flowers for the lady who was to discuss our case. Secondly, she

Paul and Gheorgie fetching water for the family

Men at work

Gheorgie with his family of geese

Dorin has a birthday treat

Water has arrived at the house!

New plastic windows are fitted

Eric and Didi admire a treasure from Didi's archive

Daniela, Robert and Hannah admire her boys' handicraft.

Beautiful Romania

A typical Gypsy King house

Dorin tries out the new loo for size

Party in Giurcani to celebrate Rita's 21 years in Romania

Rita and Boys 2005

Daniel and Alina Manole

Gheorgie's new swing

A sunny day in Iasi

explained to Eric, there was a huge benefit to be gained by him kissing the lady's hand when greeting her for the first time. I laughed. This had to be a joke. But apparently it is considered an act of respect to women in high office in Romania. I announced he should kiss her hand ten times if it got us what we'd come for. Sadly for us, we had no smart clothes with which to impress her but Daniela assured us that being English was more than good enough.

We waited an hour and ten minutes over the appointed time for the meeting. Seated in a grim, concrete corridor in a building still under construction, the head-throbbing noise from a jack-hammer prevented any conversation. I guessed a cup of coffee was out of the question.

Eventually a sassy young lady dressed in a smart business suit came out of the nearest office door. In perfect English she apologised for the delay and introductions were made. Daniela offered the flowers with a thousand words of rapid Romanian. If I'd asked what she said, she would have told me they had simply said, 'hello'. I'd long ago learned that a thousand words of Romanian are needed where ten English would cover it. Sadly, as we spent more time with Daniela I became lazy with my spoken Romanian and relied more and more on her perfect translating skills. I struggled to follow the rapid dialogue.

And then, to my amazement, my wonderful husband stepped forward with his rehearsed greeting. Not only did he kiss the important lady's hand, but looked into her eyes and told her he was 'charmed to meet her.' I'd have given him an Oscar on the spot! We were invited into her office and the long-awaited coffee was ordered from her secretary.

This senior member of the Child Protection Team told us she had never heard of foreigners taking responsibility for camine children. Consequently, she had no idea of the required procedure. She listened with interest to our plans and clearly found them bemusing. She had no idea of the status of Dorin or Adrian, she told us. The records were unclear. She pondered the question: were they adults or were they minors? She promised to make enquiries and agreed that she would give all the relevant information to Daniela. She emphasised that this would be a commitment for life, should we be allowed to take the boys into an Independent Living Scheme.

As it turned out, the paperwork for Adrian and Dorin was relatively easy to untangle when it was established they were technically still minors and, as such, under her jurisdiction. Vast amounts of paperwork needed to be signed, but eventually it was agreed that in our own time we could take the two boys out of the camine. Importantly, she agreed to leave Adrian and Dorin in Giurcani while we tried to progress our plans.

We celebrated with lunch in a local hotel and, for the first time, I really believed we could do this.

****

It was soon time to return home to Scilly. We were immensely grateful to Daniela for all her support and took her back to Iasi where she needed to catch up with her own work commitments.

156

Leaving the camine was always an emotional experience for me. Every time I left I was determined to leave with some dignity, but I never achieved it. It was heart-breaking to wave goodbye to those kids, knowing the life I was leaving them to. But this time there was more than a glimmer of hope for some of them, although according to Eric it didn't prevent the 'waterworks' from me.

On our arrival home we continued to fundraise, if anything, with renewed vigour. On St. Mary's there was a group of ladies with a wonderful talent for quilting who met each week in the home of the Land Steward. Here they sewed beautiful creations from patches of colourful fabric. They asked me if we would like them to create a large quilt which could be raffled to raise money for the boys' house. I was thrilled with such a generous gesture and the completed quilt was a work of art in vibrant orange and grey. Each section had, I knew, been stitched with hope for our boys' future.

We approached our friends who ran the Airport Buffet on St. Marys and asked if they would display the quilt and sell raffle tickets for us. Theo and Cath were more than happy to do it and so the amazing work of art appeared on the wall of the cafe, carefully covered in cellophane. The money poured in from visitors as they came and went from the islands and were tempted by the striking wall hanging. The proceeds came in one pound at a time, but soon we had raised over a thousand pounds.

Chapter 15

Not long after our return home Didi contacted Daniela and asked her to tell us about a house he had found that could be suitable for the boys. It sounded perfect. It was situated on the main road through the village so would not involve the boys plodding through deep mud in winter. It had land and a garden. It only had two rooms and a kitchen but there were also two outbuildings. The cost was £3,500 sterling and after much discussion we felt able to go ahead with the purchase. Didi also had some families in mind that might be suitable to act as guardians for the boys. (He told us later that he and Tori would have been happy to do it but, with the arrival of grandchildren they had other priorities.)

We now had to tackle the Romanian legal system. Daniela visited the house and agreed with Didi it was perfect and it was therefore arranged between the parties that the purchase should go ahead. Daniela used the Power of Attorney we had given her in readiness for this moment. Knowing the village so well, I knew exactly where the house was and Eric and I were confident about the opinion of our friends.

Nothing vaguely resembling a structural survey takes place in Romania. It is the ultimate 'buyer beware' experience. Daniela set in motion the notary paperwork which expressed our intention to buy and although it sounded straightforward to purchase a small village house, it proved to be a tricky process. But we had valuable help from the Joseph Foundation in Iasi and so the future of the boys was written in stone.

Our next problem was getting the money into Romania. It was simple enough to take cash into the country but we could only buy the house in lei. Unfortunately, lei could not be purchased outside of Romania. For many years it had only been possible to exchange German marks or American dollars, but we had it on good authority that now we could safely bring in UK sterling. Due to the difficulties of transporting cash we took the money in fifty-pound notes. As we knew the banks were renowned for rejecting foreign currency that was torn, we were meticulous about taking perfect notes.

And so it was another trip to Romania – this time to view the house and to pay for it. We also needed to choose a third boy for the project and guardians for them all. It made sense to take only three boys into the house. We knew they would continue to share a bedroom, as dormitory living was all they had ever known, and we felt four boys would overcrowd the house. This visit was to be a milestone moment for us both.

When we arrived in Giurcani we received our usual warm welcome from Didi and Tori. The grapevine works rapidly in the village and it was not long before Adrian arrived at Didi's house to check that we were there. Dorin, we were told, could be found waiting for us in the garden of the new house where he was considering what crops he would grow. And so we walked the length of the village to view our pending purchase. I was beside myself with excitement. And, as expected, we found the house was perfect. Didi held the keys so we were able to have a good look around. It was clean, tidy and big enough for three boys. The garden and an additional piece of land looked adequate to make the boys self-sufficient and we were pleased with Didi's choice. But now we needed a third boy to make the little family complete.

I had long harboured dreams of finding my lovely Gheorgie. The problem was, he had been moved from Giurcani and sucked into the adult institution system. For the moment he was lost to me but the hunt for him was imminent.

****

Daniela agreed to come to the village to help interview prospective guardians. This was an important process and we had drawn up a list of questions as well as a schedule of our expectations from the houseparents. My wishes for the boys included a healthy diet, medical care, a work schedule and behaviour guidelines. We were looking for someone who understood young men and who could have a sensible but flexible approach to the mammoth task ahead. They also needed to be brave. We were looking for someone not motivated by the money we would pay them, but who had a good heart and wanted the project to succeed.

We were blessed with all of the above and the Manole family shone through for us. They were not a family I had met before as Mariana had never worked at the camine, but they had all the qualities we were looking for. The interesting thing about them was that when offered the job they took two days to consider it. We thought that was a very good sign.

We agreed to pay a salary for two years. It was pitched at local rates and would be paid every three months in advance. During the two-year period they must meet our requirements and standards – devised to make the boys self-sufficient. We wanted the lads to learn to cook and keep their house clean. We also wanted them to cultivate their land. But what we got was somewhat different.

Mariana, Paul, their son Daniel and later, his wife Alina have taken the boys into their family. The boys don't cook or wash their own clothes; Mariana and Alina do it for them. In return, the boys work not only their own land, but also the Manole land. When we raised money to buy farm animals for the boys it turned into a family affair. Meat and eggs are shared. In fact, everything is shared and the project has worked better, although very differently, than we could ever have imagined. (This was yet another example of not impressing your own standards and expectations on people in a foreign country.)

****

Before we took Daniela back to Iasi to make the final papers and pay the notary we needed to exchange our sterling for lei at the bank. And so Eric and I set off to Birlad.

We queued in the CEC Bank in the centre of town for almost half an hour with £3,500 on our persons. The queue shuffled at an endlessly slow rate and I remember how hot it was. We finally reached the teller but were shocked, yet again, by the changes taking place in Romania. To our dismay, under the latest rules for banks, the young lady behind the glass refused to take our fifty-pound notes. Now, she told us, only smaller denominations of sterling would be exchanged due to the risk of forged large-denomination currency. What a dilemma.

We left the bank dismayed as the problem seemed insurmountable. We stood on the imposing steps of the building in bright sunshine with no idea what to do next. Eventually, we decided to return to the bank and asked to speak to Didi's daughter, Larissa, who was a member of CEC bank staff. Could she help? She was unable to give us any hope of the bank changing its policy but suggested ringing her brother, Dragoş, who was now married and living in Birlad. She asked him to come and meet us.

I had become very fond of Dragoş over the years. He's a kind, funny and gentle person who works hard to provide for his family. For a short while, when he was first married, he worked in the south of France in order to bring home big wages. It was not a good experience, he told me, but it helped to set them up with a small business.

We hoped Dragoş would have an idea to help. And so he did, but it wasn't an idea we were keen on. He suggested that our only option was to go to a black market exchange which, he explained, operated on every street corner. He said he would come with us and oversee the deal but we weren't happy about it. As an ex-police officer it went against everything Eric believed in and I was just plain scared.

Further debate took place over coffee and Dragoş assured us it was common practice in Birlad. In fact, he told us, all over Romania. He gave a confident shrug and assured us we had nothing to worry about. I certainly wasn't going to fail the boys at this stage of the operation. So, when in Rome …. We could see no alternative.

We went back onto one of the main streets where Dragoş accosted a youngish man who was loitering on a street corner. I had no idea how he recognised a money-changer. After some discussion with the guy, Dragoş told us he had agreed to exchange our sterling at that day's bank rate. He would meet us around the corner where he had his car. Eric and I looked at one another and made an agreement with our eyes. It was a case of house or no house, so it was a no-brainer.

We walked in the beating sun and crossed a busy street to the appointed place. It looked like any other street – parked cars, mostly old and rusty, busy people and children kicking an old tin can around.

An invitation was offered to join the money-changer in his car. Eric and I sat in the back seat clutching our cash while much discussion took place in the front seats. Eventually a plastic carrier bag stuffed to bursting with lei was produced. Dragoş explained that we had to show the man our money, but not hand it over to him yet. The deal was done by exchanging five hundred pounds at a time, with Dragoş checking the lei against our sterling. It was like something from a film. Very cloak and dagger.

Eventually, we were all agreed that each had what they should and we shook hands and got out of the car. I looked around, fully expecting the strong arm of the law to touch my shoulder, but we waltzed down the street with no consequences.

The next day we took Daniela to Iasi. When we told her our story of the money changing she laughed and said, 'This is Romania. It's normal'. We had an appointment with the notary where the paperwork would be completed in both English and Romanian. We would have to pay for a translator and then the deed would be signed, stamped with the official Joseph Foundation stamp and the house would be ready for the boys.

That carrier bag of lei, which had been hidden in a rucksack and guarded by Eric, now found its way into the notary's office where it was duly counted. It didn't even raise an eyebrow.

I was very anxious to fully understand the clauses which ensured the house was to be kept for the boys in their lifetimes. I wanted everything to be secure and legally binding. The translator assured us that all was in order. We were given copies of the paperwork in English and Daniela kept the Romanian version. The transaction was complete.

When we returned to the village it dawned on me that I could actually go and rescue my boys from the camine. We decided that the next day would be the right time to do it but that night sleep evaded me with the sheer emotion of the moment. Never had I dared to believe this day would come, despite the hard work we had all put into making it happen. My Christian faith was underpinned in a very special way that day.

We had agreed with Mariana and Paul that the boys should spend the first few days in the family home while they acclimatised to their new life. This would be an enormous change for Dorin and Adrian and we were anxious to take things one step at a time.

Eric and I took our hire car to the camine the next morning. Adrian was called from tending to the cow and Dorin was already speeding towards us. He shouted greetings and ran as fast as his little legs would allow. We told the boys we had business to attend to with the director and left them standing outside the office while we made our way inside.

That lady wasn't happy. She used all her powers as director of the camine to tell us we couldn't take the boys away. She had no knowledge that the papers had been signed in Vaslui, she told us. We suggested that a telephone call would confirm it. She needed the boys to work the next day, she said. We couldn't just take them, she added. I have no idea how conversations were overheard but the next thing to happen confirmed the grapevine was alive and well. Dorin knocked on the office door and announced he had packed everything and was ready to go. Adrian was lurking behind him, less confident but beaming from ear to ear.

We decided to leave the director to make her telephone call and followed the boys to their salon. Very little would be taken. Adrian had a cactus in a small pot, a radio we'd given him the previous year and Dorin had a cassette player and a baseball cap which he insisted was his own property. Technically, the clothes they stood up in were the property of the State but Eric was adamant it wasn't an issue. I suggested that they said goodbye to the staff but Dorin made a very rude gesture which suggested he wouldn't be doing that. And that was how the boys made their farewell.

However, many of the staff came to see us off, giving words of advice to the boys. Some teased them about being on their best behaviour and I could see glimmers of affection.

We drove the car the short distance to Mariana's house and introduced them to one another. Of course, Mariana knew the boys by sight but this was a whole new experience for all concerned. The lads were shy and quiet as they were shown their room. The best thing for them, and I saw their eyes shine with delight, was the enormous meal that was prepared in their honour. For the first time in their entire lives they could eat until they were full. I find it hard to write those words, even years later. They had escaped the horror of the camine and had a life to look forward to without beatings or hunger.

****

Because I am very stubborn, I was determined to find Gheorgie. I needed to trace that lost boy and offer him a better life. I was sure he would fit into the project well and I couldn't rinse his smile from my thoughts. Luckily, Daniela promised to help us but it meant we had to run the gauntlet of the director again. Only she could provide information of Gheorgie's whereabouts.

As expected, she was reluctant to release the information until Daniela told her she would ring her friend, the Director of the Protection of Children in Vaslui, and tell her some paperwork had gone astray in Giurcani. This did the trick.

It was hard to track Gheorgie down as the State records were sparse but Eric, Daniela, Adrian, Dorin and I set off to Husi where it appeared Gheorgie had been transferred. But it wasn't to be easy, of course. Upon arrival we found he'd been passed on to another institution. However, there was one bright spot to come out of the mistake that took us to Husi. I was lucky enough to spot Luçica, the mother of Petico, sitting on a swing surrounded by a group of other residents. She rushed to give me a hug and I felt incredibly emotional about that poor girl. We'd spent long hours together washing and feeding children and now she was living in this hell-hole. I remember thinking that maybe one hell-hole was much the same as another but this felt like guilt playing tricks with me.

We prised information about Gheorgie from the director and set out to find yet another forsaken institution. I was wondering if we would ever find him. If our information was correct, he was living about forty miles away in an isolated hamlet. We travelled the dust roads in silence. I was beside myself with worry, afraid that he would no longer be there, either. Could he be lost forever? Children were passed around like parcels with no value given to the contents.

Suddenly, the enormity of our quest was dawning. Was I really travelling the wilds of Romania looking for a lost boy who belonged to the State? I watched the ever-present, swirling dust that prevented us from opening the car window and stayed deep in thought. Even the boys had nothing to say, seemingly sensing the tension.

There was nothing to see but hills etched with stony pathways leading into nothingness. Miles of open road. But at last the building stood out in the barren landscape. It was an old mental institution, now full of older kids from camines and adults of all ages who had nowhere else to be. It consisted of a series of concrete block buildings with a scrubby bit of lawn at the front and looked deserted in the heat of the day.

We found the office and told Adrian and Dorin to sit on the chairs outside. We entered to find a sullen secretary sitting at a vast, brown, polished wooden desk. She looked up without a smile. Daniela, again dressed to impress, spent some minutes telling the young lady what we had come for. A slightly raised tone suggested she was not being taken seriously to begin with, but eventually the director was brought to see us. He was an interesting man. Firstly, he smiled at us. We were unaccustomed to such civility. Secondly, he was helpful, or at least he was prepared to engage with finding Gheorgie. He looked at the photo I had brought and, after consideration, said he thought that maybe that boy was in his institution. He sent the secretary to find him. In the meantime Daniela had some detailed discussion with him, presumably about how we might achieve our aim. I noticed much frowning and again the raised voices. But still the director smiled.

While we were waiting for Gheorgie to be found the institute doctor arrived. Word had obviously spread about the crazy English couple who wanted to take a boy away and keep him for life. I was unable to contribute to the conversation or meet Eric's eye; I was feeling sick with anxiety. But at last Gheorgie appeared. He was dressed in old trousers and a navy jacket but his smile was unmistakable. He threw his arms around me and refused to let go. Dorin and Adrian were invited into the office and the three boys were at last reunited.

We knew that we had little chance of getting Gheorgie released that day, or even that week, but we agreed to return the following day when, hopefully, the staff would have some information about how the paperwork could be created to allow him a new life. I also wanted Daniela to have time to speak to him and to assess his reaction to our suggestion. It was important to me that he was offered the opportunity, but the decision must be his. We said our goodbyes and promised to return.

The following day we went back to see Gheorgie again but left Adrian and Dorin behind with Mariana. They were going to help her with the animals and we felt it would be good bonding time for them all.

Upon our arrival at the institution we were not met with good news. The authority said we could not take Gheorgie unless we got permission from his parents. This was preposterous. We had no idea he had parents, let alone where to find them. Eventually 'Miss Psychologist' persuaded the director to break the rules and reveal their whereabouts.

Daniela and I did our best to make sure Gheorgie understood what we planned for him. We needed to know that he wanted to return to Giurcani, but it was hard to decide just how much he had absorbed. He was so excited. He kept agreeing with everything we said to him. Yes, he wanted to live with Dorin and Adrian. Yes he wanted to live in a small house instead of an institution. Of course he did.

Daniela was anxious to spend some time alone with him. She wanted to assess him in the same way she had the other two. She, like all of us, didn't want him to be unhappy or unable to cope with life outside of the confines of the system he'd always known. So we all took a walk and Gheorgie gradually calmed down. He appeared to have a serious talk with Daniela and answered a lot of questions about himself and the things he could remember about Giurcani. He also told us a little about his life in the institution. I wanted to scoop him up and take him home that day when I heard how he was being treated.

****

Finding Gheorgie's family would have been impossible without Daniela. She used her professional knowledge to ring the mayor's office in the town where Gheorgie was born and made enquiries on our behalf. It transpired that Gheorgie's father and a brother were known to the social worker and she kindly offered to meet with us and facilitate the introduction necessary to get consent. As the village was several hours drive away, we would have to wait until the next day. Another day lost, I thought. My patience was strung out like a violin string.

The next day we were welcomed to the Mayor's office and told that Gheorgie's father would be found tending cows in a nearby meadow. The helpful social worker gave us some background to the family circumstances which didn't make pretty reading. There were three other brothers, all illiterate, and the mother was in a mental institution.

Daniela was, of course, dressed in professional mode; we were in our jeans and T- shirts. It was with some amusement that Eric and I sat in the car adjacent to the pastureland where the father was expected to be found. We watched Daniela pick her way around the cow pats in her high heels, tight black skirt and professional white blouse and make her way to the figures in the distance. Large sunglasses shaded her eyes and, not for the first time, we remarked how lucky we were to have met her.

As it turned out, one of Gheorgie's brothers was in the field with his father. If they were amazed at the sight of visitors, they didn't show it. We watched from the car as they listened intently to Daniela. She told them of the opportunity for Gheorgie and the need for his father to give it his blessing. The brother, who bore remarkable resemblance to Gheorgie asked, 'Is my brother so crazy that he can't live with us?' Having been told of the family circumstances, which included a father unable to cope with even simple tasks around the home, the caring brother was told that it would be best for Gheorgie to start a new life with his friends. Daniela told him that the family would be given his address and be made very welcome if they wished to visit. The father was visibly upset and, with tears in his eyes, he agreed to sign the paperwork. We would, it seemed, be able to rescue his son from the institution. A large X was duly made on the dotted line. It was yet another emotional moment for me.

After years of believing Gheorgie was an orphan, I now held knowledge to the contrary. Did that mean the other boys have parents too, I wondered.

The kindly social worker took details from us of the whereabouts of Gheorgie and countersigned the paperwork in triplicate. She too had a rubber stamp. So, with the necessary paperwork in hand we returned to the institute and made our bid to have Gheorgie released.

He was again happy to see us and had not changed his mind about joining the project. His smile could have lit up a night sky and he was constantly hugging me. On this trip, we took Dorin and Adrian with us.

We were all ushered into the director's office where he proceeded to start the paperwork. It was the first and last time we witnessed a system whereby each sheet of A4 paper had to be logged, by number, in a file. It took eight sheets of A4 to complete the process and we had to sign each one. All were, of course, duly stamped with the ubiquitous ink stamp found in every State organisation in Romania. (Even today the Romanians have a propensity to stamp every document they can lay their hands on.) Rather naively, I asked if he should go and fetch his belongings. I was told he had everything on his person; in other words, he owned nothing in the world. I was shocked, despite the number of years I had worked in Romania - I have no idea why. Luckily, staff didn't ask for the clothes he was wearing to be left behind. That day I watched a young man leave a lifetime of confinement behind him and not one person shook his hand or wished him well. We just walked away with him.

****

Gheorgie

One day, just like most mornings, I was sweeping the dining-room floor and laying the tables for dinner. So I didn't see them arrive. Suddenly a kid I was friendly with said some foreign people with two Romanian kids were talking about 'looking for Gheorgie'. He said they had a photo of the Gheorgie they were looking for. He said he thought it was me. I wondered if I was in trouble.

It turned out the visitors had gone into the director's office and the doctor had been seen heading that way, too. After a while, one of the women came to find me and told me to go to the office. I was starting to feel a bit scared if I'm honest 'cos I couldn't think why foreigners would be looking for me.

The first thing I saw was Dorin, sitting on a chair outside the office. I'd forgotten how little his legs are. They didn't even reach the floor. Then I noticed Adrian. We all hugged and had a quick chat 'cos we hadn't seen each other for ages. Then the door opened and I was told to go in. My hands were shaking and I nearly ran away. But I was brave. And it was such a shock. Um... Rita was standing there with some people I'd never seen before and I rushed in and gave her a huge hug too. The director said, 'I suppose he must be the boy you are looking for,' and Rita cried. Just like she used to when she had to go back to England and leave us in the camine in Giurcani. So I wasn't in trouble after all. I don't really remember much of what happened after that. There was someone called Daniela who was Romanian. I

174

didn't know her but she seemed kind. They went away that day but came back soon.

Rita wanted to take me away and let me live with Dorin and Adrian in a proper house in Guircani. I couldn't understand properly what they meant. How could I live in a house like ordinary people? With me being handicapped. They stayed for ages the second day and I said I'd like to do what they said. Living with Dorin and Adrian again. But then they said they had to go away for a while. They had something they had to do, I think. They said they would be back soon to take me away forever. I don't know why I couldn't go that day but I just couldn't. I knew that if Rita said she would come back then she would. But it might be a long time 'cos I knew she had a very busy life in another country. I didn't mind waiting.

When Eric and Rita came for me I was excited. I hadn't been in Giurcani for ages and Dorin kept telling me we weren't living in the camine anymore. He said we had our own house with a garden in the village. I didn't believe him but it's not much use arguing with Dorin, so I said nothing. I just waited to see what would happen.

I was taken to Mariana's house. I didn't know her but she came out to meet us and everyone was talking at once. It gave me a bit of a headache. I don't like it when people talk loudly around me. I always think I've done something wrong. I remember we had a huge meal. Adrian and Dorin had been living with Mariana for over a week and they told me we had this much food every day and always meat and cheese, which we never saw in the camine. I think I was quiet that night. It was all very confusing and I *couldn't stop thinking about not ever going back to Maeliesti 'cos I had a girlfriend there. I didn't tell anybody what I was thinking. After we'd eaten we went to look at the new house.*

****

When we got back to Mariana's house there was much excitement. The boys ate a huge supper and then Mariana got the clippers out. Contrary to me believing Gheorgie brought nothing with him, it appeared he had a substantial infestation of body lice which were duly dealt with.

The following day we found Paul and the boys working on their new home. It was decided that it needed painting inside and out and they were doing preparation work for the 'paintfest.' We agreed that they should take the horse and cart to Murgeni and buy the paint and we would follow in the car. The boys chose the colours and we returned with everything needed to do the job. They had their first lesson in the intricacies of filling holes with putty and painting window frames from Eric.

We were keen for the houseparents to be involved in choosing the contents for the house and this required a trip to Birlad. It was agreed we would take Mariana and Daniela in the car and Paul would set out early in the morning in the cart with the boys. We expected to hire a lorry to deliver the long list of items needed.

Shopping with the boys was fun. We purchased everything from beds, mattresses, carpets, lino, a fridge-freezer, three-piece suite and pots, pans and cutlery. The list seemed endless, but there was no stone unturned to do the deals. We included a colour television which was the

176

highlight of their day. A lorry was hired with the help of our friend Dragoş and it made a steady journey to Giurcani, laden like a Steptoe and Son cart.

On the way home we stopped at Murgeni where we purchased chicken wire, a hammer and nails, a spade, fork and wheelbarrow and various other essentials. Every nail was invoiced and every receipt was stamped in triplicate – of course.

We were all exhausted but happy. I looked at 'my boys' and felt a swell of emotion. How proud I was of them for their courage, trust and excellent behaviour. But I was still aware of the big tasks ahead.

****

Eric

When I married Rita in 1996 I had no idea that, within a few years, I would be travelling in and out of Romania with the ease of a local. If anyone had told me I was also destined to be surrogate father to three young men from a Romanian institution, I would have laughed at the very idea of it.

Rita and I have known one another almost forty years so our marriage is based on a long-standing friendship. Her passion for orphans in Romanian was well known among our friends, many of whom were pro-active in their support. But I must confess I'd always managed to steer clear of all the hoo-ha surrounding the fundraising. Until I married her. It was just as well I had no idea about what was coming my way.

Inevitably, when Rita and I became a couple I started visiting Romania. I was curious, of course, but I also wanted to support Rita's passion for those youngsters. And in that far, north-eastern corner of Romania three young men in a camine told us they wanted a 'normal life'. There was something deeply touching about that. 'Normal' to them didn't include a computer or a bike; it just meant enough food to eat each day, a little house to live in and some land to work. Because those older lads don't have the brown-eyed appeal of younger Romanian orphans and are too old for adoption or fostering schemes, they are largely forgotten. They slowly rot in institutions. With their broken teeth, under-developed bodies and spotty faces, no one gives them a second glance. Except, of course, my wife!

No one mentioned Romania's bureaucracy either. As a retired police officer I thought I could cope with most things in life. I'm a patient man. But I'd never taken on Romania! However, I learnt quickly. I'm the first to admit that Romania is not just a different culture, having watched individual sheets of blank A4 paper accounted for in a ledger by a clerical assistant, but some days you question if the bureaucrats in that country live on the same planet.

I definitely didn't expect to get sucked through the emotional mangle. But I witnessed kids being crushed until every shard of joy was squeezed out of their young lives in Romania's infamous camines. If you've ever seen a grown man scrabble in the dust to retrieve a chicken bone, just in case it has a fragment of meat left on it, then you'll understand how I got hooked. I thought I'd seen life in all its gory detail during my thirty years in the police force. But no – I'd seen nothing like this.

It's fair to say that I wouldn't have missed our visit in October 2001. This was the culmination of all the fundraising, and Rita's dream for 'her boys'. Our aim was to set three young men on the road to an independent life, leaving behind the institution they'd known.

For three weeks we watched life-changing events evolve before our eyes with excruciating slowness. We rode a roller coaster of emotions as we fought the authorities for the rights to care for Adrian, Dorin and Gheorgie. How could it prove so hard to achieve something so simple? Every conceivable obstacle was placed before us. Huge amounts of bureaucracy for three human beings that nobody wanted – except us. We prepared documents to ensure the boys could live in the house for life and we gifted the house to a foundation in Iasi that was recommended by a friend of ours from Holland. It is no exaggeration to say we travelled thousands of miles to achieve the essential paperwork.

In the overall pattern of Romanian life our small project barely merits note —particularly when you consider the thousands of children who have been left behind. But believe me, if you could see the joy and industry those lads have brought with them, you would share our delight. When we have to leave them these days, the usual flood of tears from Rita is absent. We wave goodbye to three diligent, well behaved young men who are a credit to their community.

We have nine grandchildren between us at home. Perhaps those much loved children have inherited a granny and grandpa who appear less generous than those of other children. Actually, the truth is they have grandparents who are not prepared to join the materialistic world that heaps *so much on our children. I'm sure it's a little hard to grasp the concept when you are only three or four years old, but hopefully it's an ethos they will appreciate when they're older. For then, money from us will be forthcoming to spend on education or travel. In the short-term, they receive bank statements on all major occasions so that they can keep an eye on their investments.*

****

There were various future plans for the house. We wanted to dig a new lavatory in the garden and also build a small extension to create a bathroom. Eric thought an electric boiler would be the answer in the long term, if we could get water to the property. In the meantime they would fetch churns of water from the well outside the village. Paul had his own horse and cart so that would not be a problem and probably undertaken with the help of Adrian.

We had a long-term hope that we could build or convert an outbuilding into a cheese-making room and get the boys earning a small wage for themselves. But that was all for the future. For now, everyone was brimming with excitement and high on the whole experience.

The boys really wanted to leave Mariana's and move in to their home. We, too, wanted to see them safely ensconced in the house before we had to leave. And so the monumental day came when they arranged their new possessions, chose their beds and eventually slept for the first time in their lives in their own house. We hung the Isles of Scilly Rotary pennant on their bedroom wall and explained the significance of all the money given by the members and other wonderful people.

But our problems weren't over yet. It's a legal requirement for every resident in each village to be registered with both the Mayor and the police. So we duly took the boys along to comply but, unsurprisingly, hit a major stumbling block. Gheorgie did not exist! We had asked the boys to wait outside the police station while Daniela, Eric and I ventured inside. We were greeted with nods and stares but duly listened to. Dorin and Adrian appeared on their database, we were told, and could be issued with their credentials, but not so poor Gheorgie. 'There is no such person,' we were told firmly. 'He does not exist.'

It was time for action. Eric produced his membership card for the International Police Association (something he rarely does,) and placed it on the counter with a smile. This led to deep conversations between the men about the police force and a promise that Eric would send an English police badge to the inspector who was an avid collector of police memorabilia. Suddenly, the issue with Gheorgie did not appear to be insurmountable.

The officers asked Gheorgie's date and place of birth and took his photograph. Suddenly he became a legitimate member of society. That was surely a case of getting what you need by the back door, I think. In later months we were made aware of the importance of having the appropriate paperwork when we discovered all the boys could receive a small disability allowance, a free bus pass and basic hospital treatment if they had their ID cards. Welcome to the world, Gheorgie.

We wanted to have the boys' health checked as it was possible that something nasty could be lurking, although I quietly confirmed to myself that nothing was going to halt this project.

I had a long-standing acquaintance with the local doctor through my work at the camine. A visit to her in Murgeni enabled us to discuss the various issues that were bothering me. I was concerned, after the Dan affair, about the boy's sexual behaviour. Dr Sualia said that she didn't think there was likely to be a problem. She'd known the boys for many years and had never heard of issues with any of them. She promised to keep an eye on the family and would visit Mariana regularly to check how the boys were settling in.

The boys had blood tests to check for all the nasty possibilities. Happily they were all given a clean bill of health, apart from Adrian's and Gheorgie's epilepsy. Dorin crowed that he was perfect and needed nothing. We also took Adrian to the dentist which wasn't such a pretty picture.

****

We still had a major expenditure ahead of us. The house needed stoves built in both the boys' bedroom and the kitchen. Mariana had a friend in Pecan who was the local stove builder and we visited him to discuss when he could do the work. It was important that the job was done before winter set in. The price was agreed and we gave the money to Mariana to pay him when the job was completed. We also arranged for logs to be delivered in readiness which the boys unloaded and stored in one of the outbuildings.

Eventually, we had to go home, although I wanted so much to stay longer. I longed to see everything done and, particularly, to check how the village would accept the boys. But we had to trust those we'd chosen to care for them. The Manole family told us they would complete the painting of the house and oversee that all was well for the boys. And we felt confident that they would. I left the village, for the first time ever, with no tears. Just hugs, smiles and promises to come back the following year. Our wonderful friend Daniela had to go back to work, too, but we knew Didi would also keep an eye on things. It was arranged that Daniela would visit the boys about every six weeks and email us a progress report.

****

Dorin

When we were living in our own house, Rita and Eric visited one year and promised to buy us tickets for the circus which we heard was in Vaslui. I think I was the only one who really knew what a circus was 'cos I'd seen it on TV but we were dead excited about having a night out. When we arrived on the circus site, which was in a huge field just outside Vaslui, we hung around while Eric queued for tickets. There were loads of people everywhere and we eventually went inside this huge house made of white material. Rita said it was called 'the big top', which made no sense to me.

The first thing I noticed was the camine director's family who were already inside and sitting in seats near the back. We walked straight past them. I nodded to them and they smiled at us and Eric led us to the very front seats. I couldn't believe that we had the most expensive seats and

183

that no one else was sitting in the row. People are poor in Romania and not many people have as much money as Rita and Eric. There was a huge stage built right in front of us and there was music playing and lots of loud talking from the crowd. There was also a funny smell. I can't explain what it was but it made me excited.

Suddenly the band started playing and the stage filled up with dancers and clowns and acrobats all doing different things and all smiling right at us. We hardly knew who to look at. I loved being at the front 'cos we could see everything. Nobody tall was in front of me. I looked at Adrian and he was staring at the stage with his mouth open. I nudged him to remind him to shut it. He looks really dumb when he does that.

I couldn't stop looking at the dancers. They were really pretty girls in blue costumes like the things girls wear to go swimming, but these were covered in sparkles. I'd seen Sue Ellen wear the same thing in Dallas, years ago when Rita bought us a TV. The girls had feathers on their heads and they danced right up close to us. I'd never been that close to pretty girls before and certainly not ones with hardly any clothes on. I looked at Eric and he gave me a wink. I think he liked the girls, too.

Suddenly a girl appeared with a huge snake wrapped around her body. Rita said it was a python and she looked scared of it. I'd seen pythons before on TV but had no idea how big they were in real life. The girl put the snake down and did some juggling and I noticed the snake moving towards us. I looked at Rita and I thought she was going to run out of the tent. She looked so scared, especially when the snake started to come over the edge of the stage and very close to where we were sitting. I wasn't scared, but I was pleased when the girl noticed it and put it back round her neck. Later Rita told me how pythons curl around people and squeeze them to death. I'm glad I didn't know that at the time.

Adrian couldn't take his eyes of the girls' legs. Gheorgie just liked the snake. We had a brilliant time and after the show we all had hot dogs from a man who was cooking them in a van. We were like a chattering load of monkeys on the way home but Rita didn't say 'shut up' once. We'd all had a good time.

I knew I was born in Vaslui but I didn't know exactly where. That wasn't the right time to ask about it.

****

Adrian

One year when Rita and Eric visited they took us for a day out in Iasi. We were excited. It's a long way to Iasi and we'd never been further than Birlad. They also said we could visit Daniela. We all had a bit of money saved. I wanted to buy a new shade for our bedroom light, Dorin wanted some new jogging bottoms (he can't manage buttons or zips) and Gheorgie wanted an ice cream in a restaurant. He'd seen a pretty girl eating one on TV.

We all set off early. We had chosen what to wear the night before and it was our smartest clothes. The sort we wear if there is a wedding in the village. We never have to wear other people's clothes now. I can remember when I first realised that I had new clothes. I could hardly believe it. Nobody had ever worn them before me. I felt great.

Mariana never makes us share what we wear and the wardrobe is full of clothes, some for summer and some for winter.

It took a long time to get to Iasi and the roads were very bumpy until we were nearly there. Then I noticed how there were new roads that were smooth and sounded soft under the wheels of the car. We had to stop in the forest to have a pee. Dorin is the worst. He always wants a pee but Rita never seems to mind. Eric teases us. He says we're like three old men 'cos we need to pee so much.

We first saw Iasi from the top of a hill. I had never seen anything so huge. The buildings stretched for ever and there were some big houses that must have cost a lot of money. They were like six of our house, all put together. Dorin kept asking about everything. He wants to know what everything costs. Eventually Rita told us to 'shut up.' She always says that when we keep talking and she can't think straight. We all understand the English words 'shut up'. She said it was like having three monkeys in the back of the car.

When we managed to park Eric said we would go shopping first and after we could go and look at the Palace of Culture and have a beer or an ice cream. I was thinking that maybe I would rather have a music CD than a lampshade by now, but I didn't know if I had enough money. The traffic was really noisy. I kept standing still just to look and Eric had to rescue me from being run down by the cars a couple of times. Gheorgie told me my mouth was wide open and I'd get a wasp caught in it if I wasn't careful. And there was a tram, too. It ran on lines with big electric cables on top. I'd never seen anything like it, not even on TV.

We went into a huge shop with an upstairs. It sold everything. Music machines, clothes, chairs, socks and even lottery tickets. We saw a huge moving metal thing with steps that kept appearing and before we had time to think Eric pushed us on it. I was all right. It made me laugh, but Dorin nearly had a fit. He wobbled and tried to get his balance and Rita grabbed hold of him and laughed so much she had tears on her face. Dorin said 'uppa,' but I knew he was scared. It takes a lot to scare Dorin but that scared him. It was moving up quite fast. The worst bit was at the top 'cos none of us knew how to get off. Rita shouted 'uppa' and grabbed Dorin. Eric gave me and Gheorgie a push and then we were off. If I'm honest, I was a bit scared, too, but I didn't show it. Rita said it was the funniest thing she'd seen in a long time and was still laughing when we started looking for Dorin's joggers.

We bought loads more than we came for – trainers for Dorin which are always tricky 'cos his feet aren't really feet at all, some new cushions for the house, six music CDs which I didn't have to use my money on and some batteries which Eric remembered we needed for the TV controller. By this time we were feeling a bit tired. I think it was all the noise and new things to look at, but I felt as if I'd worked in the field all day and it wasn't even dinner time. I didn't say how I felt though 'cos I didn't want the day to end. I'd never even dreamed about a day like this.

Rita told us we were going to meet Daniela and have something to eat. I hadn't thought about food 'cos Mariana made sure we had a big breakfast, but as soon as it was mentioned I was hungry.

Gheorgie

I didn't like Iasi. I liked the trip – all of us together was fun but I was scared in Iasi. I bet no one has ever seen a bigger place in all the world. I didn't like the noise. It gave me a headache. And so much traffic was like hell. Umm...I like being with the animals at home best. Quietly. I like sitting with them, feeding them and making sure they aren't hurt. I could have stayed at home with Mariana but Dorin made me go. He said Rita and Eric would be disappointed if I didn't go but I thought they would be OK about it. Anyway, I never go against what Dorin says, so I went.

We visited a restaurant in Iasi and Daniela arrived. We hadn't seen her for ages. I like Daniela. She talks our language and always wants to know if we have any problems. Sometimes Rita talks in English and Daniela tells us in Romanian 'cos Rita's Romanian is funny. We understand her but she says things funny. When she has something serious to say to us she sits us down and makes us listen. If Dorin interrupts (he always does that) she says 'shut up' and he does. We have a lot of respect for Rita and Eric 'cos they saved us from the camines and gave us our house. Every Christmas we have a drink and say 'Narok' to them for our new life. I'd like to see where they live in England but I wouldn't like the journey, so I can't go. Even if Mariana gives me a pill I still feel sick in a car, so I don't think I'd like an aeroplane. That would be real scary.

When we got back home I was pleased I'd been 'cos lots of the village kids wanted to know all about it. They'd never been so far and wanted to know all about the moving staircase. Rita told Mariana and Paul all about it when we got home and she laughed about it all over again. I like it when she laughs. She often gives me a hug and tells me I'm special. No one else ever said I was special – only Rita. Everybody used to tell me I was handicapped or mad when I was in a camine.

****

Dorin

The first time we went to Iasi with Rita and Eric was great. We've been lots of time since but the first time is the one I remember. I wanted to ask lots of questions but Adrian told me to wait and see. Rita told us there would be lots of traffic, lots of shops and that we had to stay close to her and Eric so that we would be safe. She didn't say what we would be safe from but I thought maybe there were lots of gypsies there and they would try to steal from us. When they come to the village everybody goes indoors and locks everything up.

I was a bit worried about the long journey 'cos I always need a pee. I know Eric never minds stopping for me but it can be a bit embarrassing. Anyway – we stopped in the woods and Eric had a pee, too, so I felt better about it. It was a nice day but it had rained overnight and we had to scrape the mud from our shoes before we got back in the car.

I knew what Iasi would look like because I always watch the news and it's often on TV. There's a lot of crime in Iasi. People nick cars and things. I'd seen some very smart people too, wearing suits and dresses. I suppose it was bigger than I thought and the shops were huge. I didn't *think they would sell all that much stuff – not even in ten years. We went into the biggest shop of all. Rita said it was called a departmental shop but I'd never heard of that. We went up a moving staircase. I was OK but Adrian and Gheorgie were scared of it. Rita held on to me but she didn't have to. I was OK.*

We bought lots of stuff. Rita and Eric paid for everything and we didn't have to spend our own money. I don't think we had enough to buy very much, anyway.

When we went to meet Daniela I wanted to drink a beer with her. She comes to see us lots of times when Rita and Eric are in England and she's always kind to us. She asks us lots of questions, often the same ones each time she comes. Perhaps she forgets the answers.

Before we went home we went to the fair. Now that was good. Lots of music; things moving around that made me feel dizzy and a smell that made me hungry. We had burgers, just like in films. Gheorgie wanted some pink fluffy stuff on a stick. He behaves like a kid sometimes. Adrian kept wandering off. No matter how often Eric told him to stay close he didn't remember. Eric asked if we wanted a ride on something. I said no. What I was really thinking was that I'd like a ride on a roundabout. I wanted to sit in the fire engine but I could see it was for little kids. Rita said she would take us on the waltzers if we wanted. We all said no but now I wish we had 'cos I've never been to a fair since. I think we were scared. I wouldn't be scared now.

****

Adrian

One day Rita and Eric said we were going to Iasi again. I think Dorin needed some new clothes and Gheorgie had some birthday money to spend. I love going to Iasi, but this trip was different. We were going to meet Daniela, which is always nice. I love looking around her flat 'cos she has nice things and doesn't mind us looking. And we always go out for a pizza and a beer. I feel like a proper person when we go to a restaurant. The waiters have no idea I was in a camine and sometimes they even call me 'sir'.

This day Daniela said we were going to work with her. I knew she worked with street kids so I was curious about what we were going to do. Dorin wanted to know everything, even before we set out. Daniela smiled and told him to wait and see.

We went in the car to another area of Iasi. First I noticed lots of rubbish around and then we turned into a street where I was shocked. None of the buildings had any windows and there were black fire marks up the outside. Lots of kids were running around with no shoes and snotty noses. I hadn't seen kids like that since I left the camine.

Daniela said she had to go inside to see a boy who lived there. I offered to look after the car 'cos I thought it would have its wheels taken if we left it. Eric said he'd stay behind so that I could go inside. He'd been there before.

Inside there were no stairs and Daniela said all the wood had been burnt to keep the people warm. Lots of people were squatting around the walls. They were sitting on piles of rags 'cos there was no furniture. There was a smell of burnt wood and poo. They didn't have a lavatory, I suppose.

Dorin kept talking and talking. He wanted to know everything. Daniela told us that she visited the building a lot and there were three children living there who she had managed to get to school. One had stopped going, so she wanted to see if there was a problem.

We waited while she asked around about the boy. Someone said he didn't live there anymore. I could see it worried Daniela. She found a man sitting on a window ledge and had a long conversation with him and then she got cross. She was telling him she had to speak to the boy. I think the man was his father. After a while the man jumped down off the window and took Daniela out into the street. Rita said we could follow her.

We found the boy. He was in another burnt-out house, curled up in a corner with a dog. When Daniela spoke to him he didn't want to get up. She made him and he had a black eye, bruises all over his chest and he couldn't move his arm. Daniela was threatening the man with the police. She was furious. You don't want to tangle with Daniela when she's furious! After a few minutes she told the father she was taking the boy to hospital. The father shouted that she should mind her own business. He said he hoped she had money to pay the hospital 'cos she'd get nothing from him.

The boy had a broken arm and it was plastered up. Daniela had to pay for it but I think I saw Eric give her money. There was a lot of discussion about what to do with the boy.

Daniela said she would take him to the Joseph house where he would be looked after until his arm was better. She said she would go back another day to see his father. I bet he got a good telling off from her. She said parents *aren't allowed to beat their kids 'cos there is a law to protect them. I was surprised about that. I guess it didn't apply to camines.*

Then we went shopping.

****

For many years Dorin had expressed an interest in his birth family. He had some vague details gained from the director of the camine and knew that his family lived in Vaslui. Each time Daniela visited the village he asked her if she would help him find them. It was curiosity rather than a desire to live with them as he was very settled and happy in the house. Daniela eventually discussed the possibility with Eric and me and told us that his family address was on the paperwork that she received when he left the camine.

We gave it a lot of thought and couldn't decide if it would be in his best interests, so it was put on hold while we thought about it further. I worried about the effect it might have on the other two if Dorin's family became a reality. However, in the spring of 2007 when I made the trip to Giurcani with my son Robert, who had just become a trustee of the charity, Dorin was insistent that we take him to find his family.

We asked Daniela if she would talk to Dorin and be sure that he understood the worst-case scenario; that he may be rejected on the doorstep. As an adopted child who searched for and found her birth mother, (that introduction was made on a doorstep too,) I was well aware of the urges that he was experiencing. I didn't have the heart to refuse him. And so we set off one day, taking Daniela with us to translate.

His family lived in a high-rise apartment and we picked our way up the dark and dirty, concrete stairwell, taking care over broken steps and avoiding the litter blown in by the biting wind. Dorin was ahead of us all, clearly a man on a mission but my heart and head were full of trepidation for him.

The door of the apartment was opened by a young woman who told Daniela that her mother was out in the town, doing some shopping. She had a face so like Dorin that it left me in no doubt we had found the right family. Daniela clearly didn't believe the girl and went to great lengths to explain that we were not a debt collector or anyone bringing bad news. She went on to tell the girl that we had brought Dorin to see the family. She elaborated that he didn't want anything from them – just to meet them. Eventually the mother poked her head around the door and invited us in.

The reunion was poignant, for Dorin and for me. Dorin's mother was clearly emotional to see him. She put her arm around him and peered at him as if she was short-sighted. I don't know whose heart was beating the loudest in that room. The air was charged with emotion you could taste.

His mother explained to Dorin that she had been given no choices when she gave birth to a deformed baby. She and her husband were living with her mother-in-law at the time and much pressure was brought to bear to get rid of him. Everyone had been indoctrinated under the rule of Ceausescu to treat children with imperfections as unacceptable and it was the law that such children were hidden away in camines. They had no place in the dictator's scheme to build a 'perfect race' which he pursued with all the vehemence of Hitler. Dorin's mother told us she had fought her mother-in-law and husband for as long as she could, but eventually Dorin had to go away.

We were served coffee in a very clean and welcoming home. There were two sisters in the house that day, a husband and two small babies. They chatted to Dorin with a friendliness that was heart-warming. The mother produced a box of photos and showed us one of Dorin as a baby. She explained that she'd managed to keep him for almost two years, until she was again pregnant. Then the family forced her to take Dorin to Giurcani. Here he was left to the tender mercy of the State system, but she told us, she visited him for a while, making the long journey as often as she could. As her family grew, she found it impossible to travel the distance to Giurcani. She told us she'd eventually divorced the drunken, violent husband and brought her family up as a single mother, happy to be away from the influences of him and her mother-in-law.

We told her that Dorin was now living in his own house with two friends and that Eric and I had taken responsibility for him for his lifetime. She appeared relieved that he now had a happy life. When we left there were promises made to stay in touch which were sadly broken. The sisters told Dorin they would telephone from time to time and come and visit the village. This never happened, but Dorin took it all in his stride. He wrote them off in typical Dorin style. 'If they don't want anything to do with me then I don't want to see them either.'

It is impossible to know his true feelings but I rather think he has fed that deep longing to know his roots and now he is happy with the life he has. Interestingly, he has never mentioned them to Eric or me for several years and neither of the other boys showed any interest in his experience.

Chapter 16

I have been privileged to enjoy many family occasions in the village with people I've become attached to over the years. Probably the most colourful and exciting of these are Romanian weddings. They are richly textured celebrations and offer a feast of mammoth proportions. Traditional music is provided for dancing and alcohol is at the centre of the festivities. These typically Latin-style, exuberant affairs often last for two or three days. There is much singing and dancing into the early hours of the mornings and huge amounts of food and drink are consumed.

The services take place in the village church and in Giurcani the bride and groom walk to church together, stopping to receive good wishes on the way. Most of the families walk behind and there is a real sense of occasion. On arrival at the church, (Russian Orthodox) the bride and groom are led in circles around the altar and the priest does a lot of chanting of prayers while wafting pungent incense around with gusto. There are very few seats in Romanian churches and most people stand to watch the ceremony. Crowns are placed on the heads of the newly-weds and then prayers are said for a long and happy life together. There is an exchange of rings at some point.

Probably less spectacular, but still of interest for westerners, are the Orthodox funerals. Much importance is placed on family and friends viewing the body in an open coffin and flowers are placed around it. Often, bodies are carried around the town on trucks or carts with the bodies displayed amid a profusion of flowers. Black clothes are worn as a mark of respect and many women wear veils over their faces. I noticed that for both weddings and funerals there is kudos for the family if the occasion is attended by foreigners.

I have also had the good fortune to visit many different areas of Romania over the last twenty-two years. It is a beautiful country but its crowning glory must be the Carpathian Mountains which stretch from east to west. They do, however, contribute to very difficult journeys when trying to reach Giurcani overland.

Eric and I have travelled in and out of the country by just about every transport possible. We have flown in to Bucharest and taken the dreary train journey to Birlad more times than we can remember. We have travelled overland by motorbike twice, taken our own car about four times and latterly we took our motor-home across Europe and into Romania which caused huge excitement in the village. All of our journeys have been interesting, some scary and some exciting.

One journey I remember was the first time we rode out on the motorbike. My husband is very proud of his succession of BMW touring bikes, a habit acquired in the police force, and they make for a comfortable ride for me.

We rode through Europe without a hitch until we came to the Romanian border-post at Oradea where we met the usual chaos; hundreds of people, cars, lorries and vans all trying to get into the country. The visa and checkpoint personnel used to be some of the most corrupt and rude people I'd ever met. They were blatant about their expectations of money, cigarettes or other luxury goods should you wish to spend less than six hours waiting. The wait for the uninitiated, or those unable to proffer bribes, could be all day – anything up to fourteen hours. Over the years we'd learnt to put aside our good intent to never condone bribes and head for the front of the queue. Anyone on English plates was gazed at with awe and our spoken English, our smart BMW motorbike and Eric's retired police ID always did the trick. There were enough other issues to riddle me with guilt in Romania and I refused to allow those little episodes to become one of them.

On this particular occasion we decided to stay in a hotel about ten miles inside the Romanian border where there was no garage space available for the bike. We knew well enough the risks if we left it unattended, particularly overnight. Good locking systems would be no deterrent and the chances of us having a bike to continue the journey the next day were slim. But the friendly man on the reception desk told us that for ten US dollars (or the equivalent) they had a member of staff who would guard the bike all night. This looked like a good option, so the man was paid and we promised him a tip in the morning if he did a good job. And indeed the bike was safe.

We set off after a good breakfast on a glorious summer day for the anticipated ride through the Carpathians. I am a keen photographer and always carry a small camera on the back of the bike. Indeed, I have achieved some of my best photos that way. I remember how awed I was by the glorious scenery, all the trees in full-blown leaf sporting every imaginable shade of green. The deep pine forest made way for deciduous woodland and the wild flowers were a profusion of colour, matched only by the costumes of the many gypsy women we saw along the way.

As we travelled we saw huge amounts of house building. A good sign we felt – a suggestion that the economy was improving. In the poorer areas the new houses were being constructed of traditional mud and straw, but many people had also started using modern methods of blocks or brick. Since the death of Ceausescu people had been given pieces of land to enable them to make a new start to their lives.

Evening drew near on this particular day and Eric announced that we would stop at the next fuel station and should then start looking for somewhere to stay. The petrol station was easy to find and we duly pulled in to fuel up. There was some discussion between the garage staff and Eric about which fuel should be put into the bike. Our limited Romanian vocabulary didn't run to defining the different grades of fuel. All the pumps had black hoses so there was no colour coding to help us either. Eventually, our needs were decided by the operator on the pumps and we set off into an amazing sunset.

As the rosy glow in the sky gradually turned to a crimson fire I tapped Eric on the shoulder to ask if he would stop for me to takes photos. There was a silence from the front. I peered around his helmet and asked if he'd heard my request. A sharp voice called back, 'If I bloody well stop we'll never get going again. I've got the wrong fuel in the bike and she's coughing like hell.' Never one to notice the finer points of an engine, I had been oblivious to his anxious concerns for the last fifty miles or so. He decided to keep the bike going until the fuel was low and then top up with the right petrol. I never got my sunset photos and we travelled well into the night, stopping only when we found a rare, all-night garage. Luckily we had previously taken on fuel when the bike was still half full, always erring on the side of caution, and we hoped the mixture of the two fuels would see us through. It did. The thought of being marooned in the wilds of the Carpathians didn't sit easily on the mind and I couldn't forget our near miss for weeks.

Another bike journey was done in August 2002. My younger son Robert had married Katherine in the beautiful Cardinham church in Cornwall on a glorious, blue-sky day. We'd decided to let our guest house in Scilly on a self-catering basis for six weeks that year so that we could attend the wedding and then visit the boys. And so, we set off after the celebrations in glorious summer weather, happy for our newly-weds and full of anticipation about our bike trip through Europe.

All bikers learn the art of travelling light and we had just one pannier of belongings each – all light weight summer clothes as Romanian summers can reach 40 degrees. It was Eric's first summertime visit to Romania and the expectation was for wall-to-wall sunshine. Little did we know that this would be the summer that torrential rains hit Europe, doing untold damage to historic architecture and treasures, particularly to Prague and Venice.

Our journey to Giurcani was uneventful. Romania unfolded further layers of her amazing countryside to us – there is always something new to see in this fascinating country. I remember the Gypsy Kings' houses with shining silver roofs, colourful paintwork and ornate gardens; the poverty still marching through the villages and small children waving from the rutted roadsides as we flew through the Carpathians. There is something magical about motorbike riding – smells fill your senses until you are bursting with the amalgamated flavours of the world.

We had a lovely time, as always with the boys and spent most of our days buying yet more essentials, painting the house again with their help and watching Mariana make light work of bottling and preserving the harvest of peppers, cucumbers, tomatoes and plums. She is a wizard at providing for her family from the home-grown crops. And we noticed that the village was accepting the boys. We had no reports from Mariana of theft or unpleasantness and we saw that an easy relationship existed when the lads were around the village.

Dorin told us that they needed plastic windows in their house. Apparently, two houses in the village had installed them and he coveted them with a vengeance. He'd spent much time asking about every detail. How much did they cost, were they 'good'? Where did they come from, could anyone have them? We told him he could leave them on his 'dream list' as we only had money for essentials. It appeared to satisfy him, for that year at least.

The village roads threw dirt in our faces as is usual during summer months. I had forgotten just how bad it could be, particularly on the bike. It feels as though your eyes, nose and mouth are constantly full of grit and it's not unusual to develop a dry cough. But we had a good time.

We stayed with our friends Didi and Tori and got involved in the life of the village. Every time we return to Giurcani we have to make a dozen or so house visits to catch up with different families, all of whom have offered us kindness and hospitality over the years. Everyone wants to hear our news and tell us bits of gossip from around the community. Each year there has been a wedding or a birth. And often, more than one funeral. Children have grown and many gone off to college, much to the pride of their parents.

Our houseparents gave good reports of the boys. A little concern was expressed about Adrian drinking too much wine but it was nothing they couldn't deal with, they assured us. Their son Daniel was home from college that year with his girlfriend Alina and I was pleased to see that his relationship with the boys was easy and friendly too. Daniela, as usual, visited the village to see us.

After a wonderful two weeks we eventually said our goodbyes. We set off on the long journey home, pleased to be travelling in the wonderful summer weather. I love travelling by motorbike – the hippy me would eulogise about 'communing with nature.' Eric would just say it was fun. However, when we reached the Carpathian Mountains we were met with torrential downpours of rain. It was a particular worry for Eric as having a pillion passenger adds to problems in bad weather. The rain was relentless for hours.

We were at the point of deciding to wait out the weather and hoped to find a small cafe or kindly family who would offer us shelter. As we debated what course of action would be the safest we came upon yet another faceless village. A group of men were standing in the middle of the road which caused Eric to stop. We surveyed the scene and slowly grasped the fact that the road had disappeared before our eyes. The rain had washed away a huge chunk of the village street. This was a dilemma for us and also for the locals, of course.

We dismounted and joined the group of villagers who parted in amazement to see a UK registered motorbike and two strangers in their midst. I asked if there was an alternative route but received the familiar shrug suggesting they had no idea what I had said. Many of these villages have strong rural dialects and my stumbling Romanian appears to be Double Dutch to them.

Eric told me that he would try to find a way around the flood water with the bike and suggested I tried to cross the gaping hole the best way I could. We hoped to meet up on the other side. He disappeared down a side road which was muddy but not affected by the flood water and I asked a couple of guys it they would help me cross the hole. A lady never feels at her best in biking leathers and helmet. The drowned-rat look of the moment certainly undermined my self-confidence. Luckily, husband and wife met up within ten minutes and both were in one piece.

We did make it home unscathed, but it had not been the sun-drenched, overland holiday we had expected.

Chapter 17

There are two families in the village who are very special. The Rotaru family have been an incredible source of help and support for over twenty-two years. They have opened their home and their hearts to us and also to friends who have visited.

Didi was, until he retired, the head teacher of the local primary school. When government funding became available to build a new school in the year 2000 he stayed in post for an extra year to oversee the transfer of the pupils into the new building. Happily for me the school was built inside the vastly expensive metal fence in which I had invested, so many years before.

As a keeper of bees, a sculptor of wood and metal and an archaeologist of country renown, he has written several books on his Roman finds which have been published in recent years.

It was a common sight during visits to the village to watch Didi disappear over the grassy hillsides on his small, pop-pop motorcycle with a canvas bag slung over his shoulders. He has dug for Roman artefacts since his early twenties and has amassed a remarkable museum of pieces which, until the new school was built, were displayed in glass cabinets in the old classrooms. His house has always displayed Roman pots and artefacts, many painstakingly restored.

About ten years ago he asked us if we would consider sponsoring the production of a bi-annual, archaeology magazine he intended to write. He wanted to illustrate and document his collection of treasures and distribute the magazine to like-minded people. We were happy to help from our personal finances for a couple of years. And he produced a work of art, drawing the bones and other ancient items with a fine-nib pen. It took him almost a year to complete. Eventually his work was noticed by influential people and at last he received the recognition and funding he deserves. These days, he is called upon to lecture in Bucharest and other towns and cities in Romania. Many of his artefacts have been loaned to museums.

Didi's talent for creating works of art from wood, stone and metal are displayed around his home and garden which are museums in their own right. Our home, also, displays lovely gifts made by his skilled hands. If ever there was someone who flourished after the fall of communism, then he is the perfect example. He's a humble man with a multitude of talent.

In the early years Tori was the local banker in the village and she ran the branch of CEC Bank from her front room. It was weird to wake at 7.00am to hear the financial dealings of the village carried out on the other side of my bedroom wall. Now retired, she and Didi keep extraordinarily busy with their honey production and garden. They are also proud grandparents.

The Manoles are the other important village family, although they were unknown to us until 2001. They were recommended by Didi and Tori as 'good people' when we were looking for houseparents for the boys.

They were indeed 'good'. Paul, Mariana, their son Daniel and his wife Alina care for the boys in a way we could never have dreamed about. Little Lavinia, now three years old, is the first grandchild and much loved by all. They are a close-knit family who have little interest in village politics or gossip and we have grown to love and respect them.

In the early years I considered Mariana and Paul to be courageous. They took an enormous risk in agreeing to care for the boys which we always knew was not purely a monetary decision. They were, undoubtedly, motivated by a genuine desire to change camine children's lives. But some villagers, as expected, were not supportive of their ground-breaking agreement with us. Much was said, we learnt later, to dissuade Mariana from taking the lads. People tried to fill her head with doubt which made her determination even more remarkable. But she held her nerve and has been a shining example of what can be done with the right attitude and a little faith.

In recent years the responsibility for Dorin, Adrian and Gheorgie has passed to Daniel and Alina who are themselves, younger than the boys. Although Paul and Mariana have retired, they keep busy with the animals and vegetable gardens and Mariana still does much of the cooking for the family. The relationship they now have is similar to that of grandparents, which gives Adrian, Dorin and Gheorgie another layer of family.

When we appointed Paul and Mariana it was agreed that we would pay them a salary for two years but continue to support the boys for life. Over the years they have managed to reduce the amount of money needed from us, although the project will never be totally, self-sufficient.

There will always be a need for hospital bills to be paid and we are happy to offer this to the entire family. Provision of medicines and winter wood is expensive and the upkeep of the house, of course, still falls to us. However, due to hard work by the boys and trust and belief in our aims from the Manole family, we think we have created the perfect partnership.

If Guircani had been a town location I believe we would have managed to set the boys up with a small business. We had many ideas and worked hard to bring them to fruition. Originally we wanted to set up a small cheese-making business. We took cheese cultures and equipment from home and Daniel had some good ideas for starting the business after he graduated.

There was initial success. But two obstacles appeared. Firstly, the government brought in strict EU legislation regarding food preparation which brought with it massive amounts of red tape before cottage industries could sell their products. Secondly, an exceptionally hot summer and two very harsh winters wiped out the grassland needed for the cows, so little milk was produced.

We looked at starting a small shop, a shoe repair business and breeding and selling goat meat. This also fell under the demanding auspices of EU regulations. However, we eventually had to accept that in the wilds of the countryside there is little but self-sufficiency. Even Daniel, with his university degree, cannot find work in Giurcani although Alina is an English teacher at the local school. But we are not downhearted as the boys stay fully occupied.

An interesting aside regarding the Manole's trust and confidence all those years ago, is that today over fifty families in Giurcani have accepted camine children into their homes for which they receive a pittance from the government. The fostering programme was instigated after the closure of the camine in 2004. It must be said that not all are good placements. Some families have taken the children purely on monetary grounds and I fear for the conditions some of them endure. Conversely, I have seen some happy outcomes too.

****

The third person to deserve accolades is Daniela Cornestean. Without her it would not be possible to tell this story. She's a highly intelligent lady, qualified as a psychologist and fluent in the English language. However, despite her many talents her adult life has teetered on a knife-edge. She has been so poorly paid for her humanitarian work that, at times, she has lacked sufficient money to buy the basics of life. Her work for the charities in Iasi is commendable, but as she explained to us, 'it's not who you are but who you know that gets you the best jobs in Romania.'

When we first met her she lived with an elderly lady in Iasi from whom she rented one room, all she could afford with her meagre wages. Often, she had insufficient food and consequently her health suffered. But she continued to work at the Joseph Foundation, even when things got tough. There was never a guarantee that she would receive her salary at the end of each month. Often she didn't.

As the crisis in Romania slipped to the back burner in world terms, money became harder to find. This affected Daniela as both her wages and the overheads of the Joseph Foundation house relied on donations. Eventually, some six years ago, the money dried up and the directors were forced to put the children into foster homes. It was a very sad time. The house was sold as there was no way of sustaining its upkeep and the majority of staff lost their jobs. Daniela managed to stay on the meagre payroll, but at what cost to her? Even smaller wages and dreadful working conditions. For my part, I couldn't believe that private enterprise of such a high standard could slip away without trace. But it did.

The Foundation paid foster families a small allowance to take the children into their homes. The money was just enough to cover the costs of keeping each child, deliberately small in order to identify those families with a genuine desire to help. But after a few years there was no longer money for Daniela to make regular checks on their progress.

Eric approached the Isles of Scilly Rotary Club and with typical generosity they agreed to back another rescue plan. They offered money to buy diesel for the Foundation car for one year and a small wage for Daniela to continue her vital work. This kept the children safe, at least for a while.

On a personal level we have been privileged to help Daniela buy an apartment in Iasi which has given her security for life

Chapter 18

When the boys had been living in their new house for about a year I received an unexpected email from a Dutch lady I'd never met called Hannah. She said she had been to Giurcani and met the boys and was impressed with our project. Her main question was, would we share the blueprint of how we released the boys with her? She thought she could raise money in Holland through the Lions Clubs to create a similar project. I was thrilled to think that more of the camine children would have a chance of a better life. We corresponded for a few days and I explained how we had achieved getting the boys released and any other information I thought would be helpful. Her plan was to build a house in the village and take nine children out of the camine. We agreed to meet up with her the next time we visited.

Over the coming weeks Hannah kept me up to date on her progress. She managed to persuade the authorities to donate a piece of land on the edge of the camine for her to build the house. She was particularly keen to find useful employment for the children in her care, according to their capabilities.

I was impressed with Hannah and when we eventually met her my opinion didn't change. She was a very driven person and spent months in the village trying to get the house built. She was kind to our three boys too and often visited them with small gifts. It was, however, clear to me that her project had many differences from ours, and not least the scale of it. She intended to take some of the least-able children into the new house; those who would be unlikely to live independently without skilled support. She also entered into a contract with the Director in Vaslui whereby he would provide the wages for a woman to cook and clean for the children. It worked for a while but sadly the project became too expensive to support, particularly in the winter. After much heart-searching, Hannah eventually gave the house and the children back to the State. She has, however, found premises near the village from where she runs an impressive-cottage industry. Here, many young adults, previously from the camine, are gainfully employed.

Over the years we stayed in touch. One day I had an email from her saying that the water situation in the village had reached crisis point. The source was so full of harmful minerals that no one could drink it. She wanted to bring a fresh supply into the village via a series of standpipes down the main street. This was a *déjà vu* moment for me, having watched the French attempt to do the same thing, without success, many years before.

Hannah wanted us to contribute to the project which created a dilemma. We have always taken the financial decisions of our work very seriously; using donated money is a massive responsibility – more so than spending your own. So what to do now? I had been aware for some time that a water crisis in the village was imminent. We had even persuaded the Rotary Club in Iasi to attempt to bring a new source to the village several years before. Their experts had not found a way to do it.

Eric and I talked at length about the problem. Of course, water is the lifeline of every community on earth and, in my mind no one deserved it more than Giurcani. But I was anxious not to throw good money into a project that we had no control over. I knew that this was a complex problem with a high likelihood of failure. I was, however, impressed that Hannah was willing to try.

After much heart-searching we eventually reached a compromise. We told Hannah that we would contribute to her project but only when the water supply was in and working successfully. We also wanted, as part of the agreement, a water pipe laid directly on to the boys' land so that we could provide a proper bathroom for them. Hannah agreed to our terms and work started on the hillside to find the precious water.

Another visit to the village was called for when Hannah announced the job was done. I was full of admiration for this woman who had worked against the odds to squeeze clean water from a deep well that had been drilled in a remote hillside many times before. Of course, she hadn't been personally involved in the digging but I was under no illusions that without her the water would never have been found.

Our arrival in Giurcani to inspect the new water supply was met with unbridled joy by Dorin, who couldn't wait to show us their water pipe. True to her word, Hannah had organised water directly onto the boy's land and we were thrilled. We arranged to make the agreed donation to Hannah who, sadly, was in Holland at that time. However, the village was full of praise for her.

We arranged for a bath, basin and electric immersion heater to be fitted to provide our boys with hot water and hey presto – they had indoor facilities. It was decided that the outdoor loo needed moving again, so Eric and the boys started digging the new hole and constructed a wooden shed over it with a wooden seat. Dorin insisted that they had a sheepskin cover for the seat – ready for the winter months.

We were thrilled with the way the boys and the family had settled in together. Mariana cooked twice a day, with visible effects on our chubby boys, and they still took their meals in the family home. This was not how we had envisioned it, having wanted the boys to learn to cook and look after themselves. However, as we had it explained to us, men don't cook or do housework in Romania. It was one of those moments when we had to respect the local customs. However, the boys more than compensated for this by working hard for their houseparents.

When we asked the Manoles what would be helpful for us to provide in the future, they told us more animals would be essential to support the boys. To that end we launched a 'Sponsor a Sheep or a Cow' campaign when we returned to Scilly. Yet again, we had a wonderful response and sent sufficient money to purchase various animals.

****

During the next two winters Eric and I turned our guest house into a restaurant to raise funds for the boys. We advertised that we would host functions and dinner parties for islanders and we were kept very busy. We hosted the Christmas dinner for Barclays Bank two years running, private dinner parties and endless evenings of fun, laughter and hopefully, good food. I was chef and Eric did a sterling job as waiter and front of house.

We continued our strawberry teas with jazz on the lawn each summer, too. It never felt as if the fundraising was hard work. Groups of willing helpers piled jam and cream on scones and poured tea from china teapots. On many occasions we enticed some of our paying guests to join in too. And we poured Pimms in the sunshine while visitors enjoyed the jazz, professionally provided by friends Theo, Cath and other musicians if they were available. Happy days.

****

In 2012 we visited Giurcani in May, hoping for good weather. It was the first year we took the campervan overland and planned to spend some time in Croatia and Italy after seeing the lads.

When we arrived in Giurcani we found the boys in good spirits. Dorin had, without doubt, put on weight, Adrian had a few more wrinkles, but so did we, and the family were fit and well. Little Lavinia was three years old and already had our boys eating out of her hands. Every time she wanted a playmate it was the boys who did the honours. Gheorgie was forever pushing her on the swing and they gave in to her every whim.

Daniel told us that the previous winter had been a very hard one for the boys. Snow had come early and it had crept through the ill-fitting, wooden windows. Dorin elaborated that it had been bitterly cold in the house and it was now time for his plastic windows. We talked about the cost with Daniel and agreed that action was needed to keep

215

the fabric of the house in good condition. To our amazement, within five days we saw the windows measured, ordered, delivered and fitted. Dorin could not have been happier and we could not have been more surprised by the speed of it all.

The fitting of plastic, double-glazed windows in Romania was a revelation. Having bought some for our own home a few years earlier we expected to order and pay for them and then ask the family to oversee the fitting some weeks after we left Romania. But not so. The windows were measured within two hours of our enquiry and duly arrived after about four days. And the fitters came to do the job armed with a chainsaw. I watched Eric shake his head in consternation as they proceeded to cut the wooden windows out and 'tidy up the hole' with the chainsaw. The fabric of the house is basically mud and straw so, on reflection, we realised it was an efficient method of working. Sadly, the fitters had no plan to make good the damage inside the house, so Daniel was called in to clear up behind them. Between Daniel and the boys the damage was repaired and the room freshened up with new paint. It looked great.

We felt it was money well spent and had peace of mind that the coming years would see the boys snug and warm.

Chapter 19

Over the years the three boys have been given encouragement to speak for themselves so that their true stories can be told. They've needed prompting at times, often reticent to tell tales to outsiders for fear of retribution. But gradually trust was built and truths have crawled out from the pit that was their younger lives. And all of it has been documented in diaries which form the basis of this book. Deciding what to include from the myriad of months we've spent together has been hard, and some things have been left out to protect them. Yes – there are things that happened to them that are just too awful to tell.

Each boy holds his own special place in my heart. If Adrian tugs at the heart strings and Gheorgie makes me want to gather him up and run away with him, then the boy that makes me laugh the most is Dorin. All of them can move me to tears or fits of laughter.

Dorin takes a keen interest in village affairs and politics. He is vociferous during the elections for the local mayor and although he doesn't have a vote he holds strong views about the merits, and otherwise, of each candidate. He is more than prepared to air them, rather too loudly at times, to anyone who will listen. Being the most able and usually the spokesman for them all, he compiles a 'wish list' which he keeps in his head until we visit. One little luxury we were happy to provide was a garden seat. Dorin dreamed about it in the early days. Amid all the budgeting for the essentials we had a little voice in our ear, constantly asking for a wooden bench. As life in a Romanian village is spent mainly outdoors during the summer months, we could understand why a little seat to sit on and watch the world go by was important to him. And so we added a table and parasol for good measure. Oh, how happy Dorin was! A good deal of posturing and chattering took place as the boys attempted to establish their place in local society. And I nearly forgot - Gheorgie had a request too – he wanted a swing in their new garden.

On occasion I've needed to check a fact or two from my diaries or ask them to expand on something I want to write about. Interestingly, I am often met with a blank look. I'm sure a psychologist would have an explanation for this loss of long-term memory, but I think it is one of the greatest blessings bestowed on them. What human being could live with such horrific memories? Adrian, Dorin and Gheorgie still live in the same village where they suffered poverty, starvation and neglect throughout their childhood. Every day they meet the women who were responsible for their miserable existence. But now they live life to the full and don't have to answer to any of them.

What is particularly impressive about these three young men is they've never felt the need to apportion blame for the cruelty and deprivation they suffered as children. I've never known them dwell on what has gone before. Instead, they have an uncanny knack of always moving their lives forward. It's this, I believe, more than anything else that has allowed them to meld to the normality of village life. Importantly, they have earned the respect of fellow villagers; those who in the past never rated them above animals in outhouses. Now, the boys have a place in the pecking order of village life, albeit near the bottom. They have the distinction of owning their own home and land and they contribute to the society around them. And I'm bursting with pride for them.

In 2012 Eric and I travelled to Giurcani to celebrate twenty-one years of supporting the village. I was touched to find the Manole family had arranged a party for me and invited many village friends to join us. And the very special guests were some of the camine boys, those who are now in foster families around the village and who I watched grow up. Now grown men with varying abilities, all are contributing in some way to village life. It was a special evening with wonderful food and good company.

There can be no end to this story as 'our boys', even as you read this, are carrying on their lives with zest and vigour. What more could Eric and I ever have hoped for? We continue to fundraise and visit, but the long-term future of 'our boys' lies with our own children and the younger generation of the Manole family. We have deep faith in them all.

We raise our glasses to you, Adrian, Gheorgie and Dorin. Narok!

****